A CELEBRATION OF
OLD ROSES

Persica Euphrates

To my two daughters, Wendy and Rhonda,
and their children

Schneekoppe

Micrugosa Deep Pink

CONTENTS

All photographs were taken by the author,
except those of Countess of Stradbroke and
Alister Clark's garden, which were taken by
Susan Irvine.

Nyveldt's White

FOREWORD

In his third book on old roses, Trevor Griffiths brings his record of species and hybrids still in cultivation to an amazing eighteen hundred. Travelling the world in search of plants which, whether historic or modern, have the old rose character, he has discovered many which are little known but have real garden value. Himself a well-known rose collector, nurseryman and hybridiser, with an extensive rose garden, he has written a book which is not only an important work of reference but is so beautifully illustrated that it may entice the amateur to grow fine roses which are outside the common run.

All the categories of the old roses with the lovely names are represented — the musks and damasks, the noisettes and centifolias, the albas and mosses, and many more. There are shrub roses, climbers and ramblers, some of certain provenance, some of unknown parentage, and yet others which are modern in date but worthy to be counted among the classics.

Trevor Griffiths is strong on the practical aspects of rose growing and discusses the placing of old roses in the garden. The giant climbers look well on posts or canopies, the shorter climbers on walls, fences or pillars, while the ramblers, with their flexible branches, may be trained over arches or along chains or ropes looped between posts. Of the shrub roses, some contrast well with evergreens, others can make a loose hedge, others bring pleasure late in the year when most hardy shrubs have finished blooming. The author also discusses scent, stamina and length of flowering season, important qualities to the amateur gardener when making selection choices.

ANNE SCOTT-JAMES
London

Sir Walter Raleigh

INTRODUCTION

Anyone who has read 'The Making of a Garden' in Trevor Griffiths' first book will have some idea of the kind of person he is, and his dedication to and love for roses. To meet him and to listen to him talk about them is even more of a revelation. I have by now met many people around the world who have devoted their lives to roses, and many of them I am proud to call my friends. Often they have a genuine love of roses, but none that I can think of have a greater love than Trevor. Very few has a greater knowledge and very few are so likeable.

To have gathered a collection of old roses as extensive as that which Trevor holds at Temuka is a considerable achievement and, when it is considered that New Zealand is a country of some three million people, to keep these available commercially is even more of an achievement. It also says a lot for the good taste and gardening knowledge of New Zealand gardeners. It should also be added that Trevor has had the devoted backing of his wife, Dixie, as well as his family, for his is a truly family enterprise.

We have been fortunate enough to have had a visit from Trevor on three different occasions, the most recent together with Dixie. It is always a pleasure to show him around our roses, and we consider ourselves very fortunate to have Trevor's nursery as main agents for our English roses in New Zealand — we know they will be appreciated and well looked after.

If one puts this book together with Trevor's first two books we have what must be the ideal introduction to the whole field of old roses, shrub roses and climbing roses: indeed, not just an introduction but an extremely valuable work of reference, interesting, authoritative and written with Trevor's typical directness, charm and enthusiasm.

DAVID AUSTIN

PART ONE

Rambling
with Roses

*If I give you a rose you will
not doubt God any more.*

Tertullian (*c.* A.D. 160-225)

La Roseraie du Parc de Bagetelle

Rambling with Roses

It could be said, 'another journey, another book'. The truth is that, not long ago, circumstances came together for us to make a wonderful trip to see rose and nursery friends across three continents. It has always been my belief that three things need to come together for journeys to be made: the time, the money and the opportunity. We were particularly fortunate that all these three came together for us. I hope that you too will benefit from our travels and experiences, and perhaps through this, your love for old roses, like ours, will be strengthened.

Identification of the old roses still seems to be the most difficult problem to solve. It is more than a little off-putting to see a rose in California given a specific name, and then come across the same rose in Denmark with a different name, and, as if this is not enough, find that self-same rose under yet another name in Germany. There will never be any one authority to whom we can refer for a decision on the naming of a rose. Those who knew have gone, and in many cases those who are left are confusing the issue. It simply is not good enough to be satisfied that the rose you have in your possession fits the description from one of the many books or catalogues that are available from years gone by. Identification is a complex subject. The worst mistake that can be made is that you should assume the name for your particular rose is the correct one and that everyone else is wrong.

It must again be emphasised that it is always very possible that the variety for which you are trying to find a name is in fact just a seedling and never had a name in the first place. This can apply to many roses found growing wild in such places as redundant churchyards or the deserted gardens of derelict farmhouses or cottages. Today one can travel through England and Scotland and see many different forms of *R. canina* — or dog rose — growing along the roadsides, from white to blush pink, through medium to deep pink, and with different-sized flowers as well. If this can happen to an accepted species of Rosa which has been in the landscape for thousands of years, then what changes can you expect in seedlings from a comparatively young rose of, say, 200 years ago? In my eyes, at least, you are doing roses and yourself a disservice if you positively identify a rose when you have even the slightest doubt that the name you are suggesting could be incorrect. It would be better left unnamed.

For some time now there has been some confusion in my mind over three roses which in recent years have become popular in New Zealand. They are 'Wedding Day', 'Rambling Rector' and 'Seagull'. My suspicions were aroused in 1984 during my travels across the United Kingdom, Western Europe and Japan. It became very obvious that 'Wedding Day' as I knew it over fifteen to twenty years was very different from the roses of that name I saw in the above countries. The rose in my collection came from a reputable English nursery. In 1985, in an attempt to clarify the situation, I imported all three rambling roses from three different countries —

'Wedding Day'

'Seagull'

'Rambling Rector'

Westfalenpark

East Germany, Denmark and England. The budwood duly arrived, was budded in the quarantine area and eventually grew well and was released for propagation purposes after the mandatory two-year period.

Without going into too much detail on the long process of cross-referencing, it now seems reasonable to assume that the real 'Wedding Day' is a wispy, gentle grower, having single white, fragrant flowers with golden stamens, in clusters. The important point is that the petals do not touch or overlap as in the variety we have known for so long. (See page 15.) 'Seagull' is not semi-double but rather single, with perhaps some small petaloides occasionally. The size of the flower is a little smaller than that of 'Wedding Day'. 'Rambling Rector' is semi-double with gold stamens, and the flower size would be the smallest of the three, at about 3 cm. The wood and growth of all three is distinctively different. This story is related so that you will realise that the naming and checking process is an ongoing, never-ending function.

If you ever get the chance to visit West Germany, mark down on your itinerary Westfalenpark, in the beautiful city of Dortmund, as a special place to visit. Its origins came from the Federal Garden Show held in 1959, when 60 hectares were developed; later a further 10 hectares were added. The park today has many attractions, including the 212-metre Florian Tower from which you can gain a fine view of the park and the countryside. There are many water areas, entertainments for adults and children, restaurants and cafés, animals to see, a miniature railway and chairlift, but of course the important part is the rose collection.

The Westfalenpark boasts some 3200 planted varieties from home and abroad. The modern roses appear to be planted in beds and groups from their country of origin, and it is marvellous to see roses here that I had thought were long

lost to cultivation. The climbing roses are in groups, and there are many types and colours that were not familiar to me. Of course, strong emphasis is placed on locally raised varieties. There is also an excellent collection of old and species roses, representing all facets of all the families.

Westfalenpark rosarium is undoubtedly a very fine unit, with its spacious lawns, pools and gardens. Those responsible for its establishment, development and maintenance must be commended, and it behoves all rose-loving visitors to West Germany to make the effort to visit this haven. Walter Steine, a director of the park, was most helpful.

Having visited the state rosarium in Sangerhausen in East Germany in 1984 with more than a little difficulty, we approached our visit there in 1988 with some trepidation. We are very happy to say that no problems arose and we were made very welcome. The director, Ingomar Lang, and assistant, Helle Brumme, were very helpful and we were shown the layout of the various gardens and then left to our own resources. My earlier visit had been out of season, but this time the roses were mostly in flower and we saw many that will eventually find their way to New Zealand.

When the rosarium was founded at Sangerhausen back in 1903, the resultant work and care put into the collection was available to everyone from all countries, but when Germany became divided after World War Two, this unique effort was no longer accessible to those in Western countries.

For the past five growing seasons we have received batches of budwood from Sangerhausen, and these have been very successful. No matter what source old roses come from, there is always an element of doubt with some of the names. We are pleased to inform rosarians that the Sangerhausen staff are carrying out a meticulous study of all their roses and the authenticity of the names. Two of the roses we will be able to make available from this source are 'Dunkelröte Tausendschön' and 'Weisse New Dawn'. Everyone knows the beauty of 'Tausendschön', and a deep-red form of it will be welcomed as an addition to the rambling family. Likewise, there will be few people who do not know the attributes of 'New Dawn', and a white form of it will be an extra pleasure. We left Sangerhausen and Erfurt, two lovely old towns, sad that our stay could not have been longer but secure in the knowledge that the people there love their roses just as we do. The large man-made mountain nearby (from a copper mine, I believe) seemed to beckon and say, 'Come again, *auf Wiedersehen.*'

One of the interesting things in life is the ability to recall incidents that have happened many years ago. Of course, the memories are sometimes sad, but at other times they may be happy. I remember walking along a country road in Denmark, between the towns of Love and Hong on the island of Zealand, on my way to meet a long-time acquaintance, Valdemar Petersen. This country road had a drainage channel in the grass verge. Without warning, a bicycle went past me, ridden by a lady, and about 20 metres further on she crossed the channel to enter a driveway to a house. My mind flashed back some thirty years or so to a similar occasion when, on my way to work one morning in my 1929 Austin Seven car, I could see not far ahead a lady on a bicycle. I knew this lady cyclist very well, and sometimes when she heard or saw me coming, she would wobble her machine, pretending she was nervous. Just as often, I would do the same, as if each of us was frightened by the other. This particular morning she looked behind her, saw me coming, wobbled her bicycle a little, crossed the grass channel and footpath and, clinging to the hedgerow, called to me as I drew level, 'Roadhog!' I could not let this opportunity pass, so spontaneously called back, 'Hedgehog!'

Some years ago now, I well remember a customer specifically asking me for three roses to climb on, or near, her house, and she was adamant that they had to be thornless. It was not in my nature to carry out this instruction without asking why they had to be thornless. The reply came back that she did not want her children to get caught up in them, and that although she wanted scented, ever-blooming roses, she definitely did not want the prickles. I asked her how many children she had and was told three. The conversation went on with my asking her if she intended to stand beside her children for the rest of their childhood and see that they never suffered any of the hurts associated with the growing years. In fact, with tongue in cheek I suggested to her that she would probably do her children more good if she pushed them into a rosebush and then they would have the greatest respect for these plants for the rest of their lives.

I have never been able to understand why people want thornless roses. To me, it is like asking for the day without sunshine, and deliberately to breed roses which are supposedly thornless seems to me to be deliberately messing with Nature. I can understand the need for hybridisation to improve things such as crops, animals and fruit, but I cannot for the life of me understand why man or woman must interfere with Nature purely for their own selfish benefit.

Sangerhausen

A perfect example of meddling with Nature is when some dairy farmers see fit to remove cows' tails. One must always remember that if one starts this meddling process in any field of endeavour, the results often produce side-effects which are not intended. Often individual roses are blamed for hurting people and animals or damaging property, but it really is not the roses' fault. The mistake is made usually by the person planting the rose. You cannot blame the plant if it finds itself in a restricted area and not given the necessary room to develop. Those who deal in roses and are engaged in their production have no more problems in handling them than the average housewife does with hot pots and dishes.

During our recent journey through Great Britain and Western Europe, one factor stood out from all others — the number of roses of all types used in what may be generally termed 'public plantings'. These countries must be a rose-grower's paradise. From a car, bus or train, the sight everywhere of thousands of roses is marvellous. Near Heathrow Airport a wide median strip includes quite mature beds of 'Frühlingsgold' and *R. rubrifolia*. The beautiful coppery-grey foliage of the latter forms a remarkable contrast with the green grass and the more distant trees and shrubs. These types of roses are very hardy and do well under the difficult conditions experienced near motorways.

In different parts of England, Wales and Scotland, beds of roses, both modern and old, are everywhere: around the perimeters of city carparks; inside and outside school grounds; in town squares and cemeteries; in the vicinity of motorway service stations, and often in the centre of major roundabouts. You will also see them near churches, cathedrals and railways stations — in fact, in almost every conceivable situation, even on a roof-top carpark.

The important thing to remember about all these plantings is that they do not have to be

A Celebration of Old Roses

Queen Mary's Rose Garden, Regent's Park

replaced for many years. They form a place of beauty and fragrance while at the same time forming an impenetrable barrier through which dogs, children and bicycles do not find it easy to pass. They really only require one annual maintenance programme and, for the initial outlay, give a lifetime of service to the community. In Denmark and Germany rugosas and shrub-climbers were used in profusion. In most cases the former never seem to be without fruit or flower, while the latter put on brave displays where you and I would not even think to plant them.

Another interesting development we observed in Denmark and Germany concerning public planting was the extensive use of *R. rugosa* and its hybrids, and the results of these plantings beside buildings like railway stations, beside bus stops, pedestrian crossings, in roadway island areas and along motorways and railway tracks. Because of this family's ability to form fertile seed and its prolific germination, it does not take very long for the original planting to thicken up and spread extensively. For kilometre after kilometre from trains, it is not difficult to see a single-line planting of rugosas, and in many places they have spread both up and down the banks. The inbuilt tenacity and durability of these roses is amazing when you think of the

effect the frequent speeding trains must have on them. They not only withstand the extremes of temperature, from very hot summers to extremely cold winters, but also the pollution associated with man's infernal machines. It seems the rugosa family of roses must be among the toughest in the plant kingdom.

While we were in California our attention was drawn to a recent article about the spread of *Rhododendron ponticum*, an increasing problem in the northern parts of the British Isles. This particular species, originally planted in many parts of Scotland and northern England, can be seen at its worst from the road alongside Loch Ness. There is no doubt that it is spreading but it is doubtful whether it will ever get further than the northern districts as it only grows well in cooler climates. But during our rose rambles through California, the United Kingdom and Western Europe I believe we saw a plant that is potentially a bigger threat than *R. ponticum*. It is *Buddleia alternifolia*, and it is present in all these countries. Although there are not many established groups of it as yet, its spread is already assured. In one of its several forms you can see it on industrial sites and adjacent to the oil wells in California. It is there in England, Scotland and Wales and it is present in Sweden, in many places in Denmark and in numerous cities in West Germany, East Germany, Italy, Switzerland, France and Belgium. The seeds are easily spread by birds, wind and water, as well as with human help. I have seen plants growing in the spoutings of tall buildings, between the cobblestones of many streets and roads, around the foundations of churches and cathedrals and even halfway up a stone wall on an old castle. The thousands of pigeons that seem to be accepted in most of the world's major cities may well be the very birds that carry the seeds of *B. alternifolia* everywhere. It goes without saying that *R. ponticum* and *B. alternifolia* will cause problems wherever roses are growing.

On my first expedition to the Northern Hemisphere rose-growers, one of my visits was to Poulsens' Rose Nursery, some distance north of Copenhagen. My instructions were to proceed by rail to a town called Hillerød and get additional transport to Kelleris. In due course the train stopped at Hillerød, and there was just myself and a well-maintained station building in sight. The taxi stand was deserted, and at the bus stop I could not understand the timetable, which obviously was written in Danish. With a feeling of desperation I turned towards the station building and yet with some hope I knocked on the door. A voice spoke in Danish, and when I asked for help, a voice in English told me to open the door. The owner of the voice was a young lady who was very helpful in telephoning both Poulsens and a taxi. After thanking her I was privileged to enjoy a most pleasant visit to Kelleris, the home of the Poulsen family.

The story now moves on twelve months, when it was necessary for me to visit Denmark again. This time from Aarhus I took the train to Hornslet, with the intention of making my way to Lykkes Rosenplanteskole at Søby. I was the only passenger to get off the train at Hornslet, and there was no taxi present at the stand. As happened the year before, I could not read the bus timetable, so my attention was again focused on the station building. As I crossed the road towards the building, an uncanny feeling of having had all this happen before came over me and, believe it or not, when I knocked on the door and asked for help, it was the same young lady who answered and made the telephone calls for me. This coincidence is all the more unusual when you realise that the two incidents took place several hundred kilometres apart. As if this story were not hard enough to believe, during our third trip we were with Danish friends when they had need to visit the post office at Hornslet, which is adjacent to the railway station, and who should be at the counter but the same young

lady. This time we found out her name was Anne.

When you are regularly dealing with the public as we do in our nursery and rose garden, you always have to be mindful of your actions and your words. If it is your wish to say or do something that would not be generally acceptable, then you have to make sure that no one is looking or listening. Usually I have no problems of this sort, but once or twice in my thirty-odd years of serving the public I have been caught out. It happened recently on a very beautiful warm day. We had just finished lunch and from our upstairs windows I could see that there was no one about at all. I descended the stairs and proceeded down the wide lawn path in the direction of the budding plot. I stopped momentarily at my small dovecot which contained five white fantail pigeons. During the preceding months the older male bird had been asserting his authority over the others, and one bird in particular seemed to be getting the most punitive attention. On many previous occasions I had interrupted what seemed to me to be unnecessarily hard treatment. As I walked close by the present fracas I commented in an ordinary tone, 'Leave her alone, you silly old b.....' To my complete and utter surprise, a man's voice replied from the damask rose section, not 20 metres away, 'I didn't touch her!' Needless to say, to my great embarrassment he appeared with his wife from behind some large rose plants. They had parked their car out on the main road, out of sight from the house, and quietly proceeded to look around the rose garden. After much merriment they went on with their inspection and I got on with my budding.

You are probably aware that the rose 'Mermaid' is generally considered to be sterile, this factor being inherited from one of its parents, *R. bracteata*. There are a few hybrids from 'Mermaid' about, which means that there must have been moments when it *was* conducive to hybridisation. One of these occasions took place some years ago near San Francisco, in Palo Alto, I believe. A large, well-established plant of 'Mermaid' apparently dropped a fertile seed head and, quite unexpectedly, five small seedlings appeared in close proximity to each other. Apparently the owner of the property was knowledgeable enough to allow the seedlings to grow and develop, and in due time they must have been shifted or propagated from and were thus preserved for some time. I do not know the exact details of the story, but it did resemble the above.

The seedlings seemed to inherit all the attributes of their parent except that they were much smaller. They all grew a little differently from each other, and as far as I know, only two of them have survived. One, called 'Happenstance', was introduced in California. It grows about a metre high and sends out young shoots about another half a metre or so. In every way it is a replica of its parent. The other surviving seedling from this fortuitous set of circumstances came into my possession from Roses of Yesterday and Today in Watsonville, California. For the want of a better name, I have called this rose 'Dwarf Mermaid', because in fact that is exactly what it is. In every conceivable way it is a true genetic dwarf of its parent. Every facet of it is a perfect reproduction of 'Mermaid' except its growth habit; it forms a compact mound of about 90 cm high and wide. When this hybrid becomes better known I am sure it will be treasured by all true rose lovers. You will see a lovely picture of it on p. 28 in the 'Species and their Hybrids' section. When we think back on the origins of 'Dwarf Mermaid' and having been able to study the plant in reality, it would appear that no other rose took part in its creation. By some freak of Mother Nature a rose that had generally been accepted as sterile suddenly placed a fertile seed pod on the ground below.

There is another little-known rose which seems to have come from 'Mermaid' as well and, strangely enough, it originated in California too. This is known as 'Pink Mermaid' and bears no resemblance to the previous one at all. The plant sends out lovely long shoots or canes which can be easily shaped or trained. It has attractive, glossy, dark-green foliage and not many thorns. It has a healthy appearance and the flowers are light pink, single and about 9 cm across. The five petals are separated from each other, or rather, do not overlap, in the manner of a clematis flower. It has one major flowering and quite a few late flowers as well. I have no idea of its parentage except that it may have some 'Tausendschön' blood in it. This, too, is illustrated later in the book. (See p. 137.)

If you ever travel to France and, more particularly, to Paris, do make an effort to visit La Roseraie du Parc de Bagatelle, situated in the Bois de Boulogne not very far away from the centre of the city. It is delightfully situated in a huge green area of several hundred hectares, which previously belonged to the Château de Bagatelle estate. Mostly flat, the garden falls away in a gentle slope on one side and on the opposite side is raised to a small gazebo-like building from which you can enjoy a panoramic view of the whole area. The rose garden is mostly formal, with regular beds edged with well kept box hedges. I suppose most of the the

varieties are modern, but there are some very well developed old roses and species there too.

A feature of the gardens are the steel supports which carry climbing or rambling roses to the majestic height of 4 metres or more. They are unique in their design and, when completely covered with mature plants in full flower, are absolutely beautiful. It makes you wonder why this method of support is not used more often in other places.

Another feature is the trial of new roses under garden conditions. To mention one rose only, it was exciting to see one of Jack Harkness's hybrids developed from R. persica doing very well here. I am aware of three hybrids in this family so far. 'Tigris', the first released, has semi-double flowers of lemon with scarlet patches deep down in the throat. 'Euphrates', the rose present in this Parisian garden, is single and of a most unusual colour. You could say it was a dull rosy salmon with the distinctive blotch deep down on each petal. The third hybrid, just named and released in 1988, is 'Nigel Hawthorne' (see p. 33). These three roses signal the arrival of new blood on the hybridising scene and we do not know what wonders lie ahead of us. Although these roses are quite new, they are old in concept.

In many corners of many countries, enthusiasts have worked on raising roses for the love of it, and in their own way they have added lustre to different families in particular and the genus in general. One of these unsung heroes is Toru Onodera from Japan. As so often happens, many people are influenced in their choice of employment or pastimes by one particular person: in Toru Onodera's case it was his mother who exerted this influence, she being a teacher of the well-known Japanese floral art form, Ikebana, and the possessor of a deeply instilled love of flowers. After the war, a geologist by profession, Toru found time to follow more leisurely pursuits and turned his attention to raising roses.

Many roses owe their origin to this devoted hybridist, and if you know him for nothing else, you will know his beautiful 'Nozomi', which is grown and loved all around the world today. It was named after his young niece who lost her life during the war. There is no doubt that 'Nozomi' was the first of a new type of rose, and when you realise it came from two miniature roses, 'Fairy Princess' and 'Sweet Fairy', and that both of these roses had 'Tom Thumb' in them, then this is indeed a breakaway. Jack Harkness refers to this rose and its close relatives as the 'Onodera-type rose'. I have in my possession three of its sister seedlings, 'Akashi', 'Suma' and

La Roseraie du Parc de Bagatelle

'Miyagino', all of which have the same growing habits as 'Nozomi' but differ in their various shades of pink. For those of you who are not familiar with this rose or its habits, it can grow quite vigorously, with dense, arching, prickly branches, and if left to its own resources will form an impenetrable mass, as can be seen in the alpine garden at the Royal Horticultural Society's gardens at Wisley. There is no doubt that this rose is being and will be used by hybridists to produce procumbent ground-cover roses.

A visit to Toru Onodera's home at Saitama outside Tokyo reveals the nature of the man and his work. The garden is lovingly put together, with roses, in particular seedlings, to the fore. It is not hard to actually feel his philosophy, 'truth and beauty are in Nature', present in this lovely spot.

On our travels throughout the countryside of Britain we were very impressed with and envious of the use of bricks everywhere. It seems they are very compatible with roses, being used for pathways, driveways, walls of all heights, archways, towers, pillars and all manner of buildings, as well as steps and stairways in all shapes and sizes. Probably it is the lovely, natural earthy colour of bricks which fits in so well with roses. The brick walls used as shelter and support adjacent to many important rose gardens are magnificent structures. It is likely most of them were built many years ago when labour and materials were relatively inexpensive. It is important to remember the tremendous

influence these walls and other structures have on roses. Firstly, they provide almost maximum shelter for the plants. A young rose, planted at the base of a wall in the case of a climber or rambler, or nearby in the case of a bush or shrub, would have immediate protection from icy blasts which can be so damaging to young, soft growth. These walls give a measure of secure support which other types of material and shelter fences can never give. Once a climbing or rambling rose is established on such a solid structure, it is there for a lifetime, with the possible exception of broken ties. These majestic constructions, reaching at times 3–4 metres high, also always retain a measure of warmth even on their exposed side, which is of paramount importance when establishing young roses in a colder climate, and when these walls are used to surround gardens, their beneficial effect is increased many times.

One beautiful rose garden which has used these walls to their best advantage is Mottisfont Abbey, near Romsey in southern England. Established in 1957 under the auspices of the National Trust, this mature garden has a fine collection of old and not-so-modern roses. One feature that stands out is the space between the plants; it is good to see them with room to develop. Wide paths and box hedges are plentiful, but it is the roses which appeal most. It seems that this collection of roses has the highest percentage of name accuracy, brought about by Graham Stuart Thomas in association with the curator.

A Celebration of Old Roses

Rose garden, Sissinghurst Castle

Sissinghurst Castle in Kent, also managed by the National Trust, is another beautiful garden where bricks are used in many ways. Sissinghurst is not really a castle, but this matters little to the thousands of visitors who enjoy the immaculate gardens each year. Although the area is perhaps small by some standards, it is the quality of the plants, and the manner in which they are used, that takes one's eye. This garden in its entirety is one of the most beautiful and said to be the most popular in the United Kingdom.

Vita Sackville-West and her husband, Sir Harold Nicolson, certainly put together a wonderful collection of plants over a period of many years. They have shown how roses and other species can be planted together. Anyone who has read the fascinating stories of the purchase of this property and the planning and the planting of it over many years, and then had the pleasure of visiting it in more recent times, knows very well what a wonderful garden it is. No one should miss visiting Sissinghurst.

I am avoiding describing roses in these gardens, because it has all been done before, but sometimes a particular feature stands out which I feel needs to be mentioned in the hope that you, the reader, may be able to use the idea. To me, this feature at Sissinghurst is the magnificent centrepiece in the white garden. It is a large metal canopy covered with several plants of *R. longicuspis*. When in full bloom, it is a glorious sight, and the heavy scent penetrates long distances from the actual area of the plants. This canopy is 8–10 metres in diameter and stands more than 4 metres high. It is supported by steel pillars with two or three metal rods in each, and a strong framework of supporting metal rods or bars holds the canopy in place. Of course, the massive growths of plants of this type weigh very heavily when in full growth, and an especially strong frame is required to carry that weight. This framework could be made from other materials, including wood; it could be larger or smaller than the one described; and many varieties of roses could be used to cover it. Some of these could be 'Wedding Day', 'Filipes Kiftsgate', *R. banksiae alba-plena* or any of the beautiful members of the rambler family.

We will now move on to the sections dealing with the individual roses. Inevitably, as we delve further back into the old roses, we find there are fewer varieties coming forward from the early families, and probably more from the later ones. Nevertheless, all the roses photographed and written about here are of the same high standard as the varieties I covered in my previous books.

La Roseraie du Parc de Bagetelle

PART TWO

The Roses

It was roses, roses all the way.
Robert Browning (1812-89)

Rousseauiorum

Species and their Hybrids

As you perhaps will be aware, two very interesting groups of species and their near-relations have already been covered in my first two volumes. Here in the third book, we have another group of extremely different species which, in their own way, make the field and the choice much wider.

One point which should be explained is that different countries seem to recognise different names for the same species. There is no doubt that, by the rules of botany, one name will have precedence, but this does not stop some countries from adopting their own chosen authority. From time to time I have been challenged by people over my choice of a name, but because I know my books find their way into many homes in many countries my choice varies, according to strict procedure, to accommodate the priorities of students of the rose everywhere.

Another aspect that I have become very conscious of in my meanderings through the beginnings of the genus Rosa is the work done by hybridists in every nook and corner of every country. Rather like the honeybee, which has the uncanny ability to make its way straight back to the hive, these hybridists, who have numbered hundreds over the years, are exceptionally good at selecting their parent plants, after which nothing can make them deviate from the line of breeding so chosen.

One of these hybridists (who, incidentally, was rather late in starting) is Jack Harkness of England. His nectar-giver has been *R. persica*. It is rather amazing that from all the roses he could have chosen, he selected probably one of the most difficult to work with. It does not set seed easily and it is not easy to hybridise.

However, from this difficult situation Jack has created superb roses, three of which appear in the list that follows. They are different, they are exciting and they show what can be done. One cannot but admire the man for electing to take on such a difficult project and, after due process, finishing with such excellent results. It also shows the way to others who, for one reason or another, might be a little faint-hearted about trying a programme which at first sight seems fairly difficult. The door is wide open to the honey pot and all that is required are the bees to travel that straight and undeviating line back to the hive. ■

▲ **Arnoldiana** (1914). Known affectionately as the 'Arnold Rose', this hybrid is believed to be a cross between *R. borboniana* and *R. rugosa*. It grows to at least 2 metres and produces large heads of crimson-purple which are semi-double and about 5 cm across. Upright habit.

▲ **Biebersteinii**. Some authorities would have this species as the same as *R. horrida*, but there are those who believe that it is different enough to be listed separately. Grows to about 1.5 metres, is very prickly and has corymbs of small white flowers. Sometimes referred to as the 'Crimean Sweetbriar'.

▼ **Borboniana** (1828). This species, if it is such, was given its name by Narcisse Desportes, a French botanist. The photograph shown here was taken in Le Parc de Bagatelle in Paris. The rose there is considered to be the original form, with very deep rose-pink double flowers. Quite fragrant.

A Celebration of Old Roses

◀ **Bracteata Mermaid Dwarf**. As this beautiful hybrid is dealt with at length elsewhere in this volume (see p. 20), I will confine myself to a description. Grows to less than 1 metre in a compact, rounded bush. When in flower it is covered with lemon-yellow single blooms about 8 cm across. Very fragrant.

▼ **Cantabrigensis Alba**. Probably most rosarians know the type but may not be familiar with this white form. There seems to be little difference in the plant from the parent, and the blooms appear in the same way, but in this instance they are pure white.

► **Cinnamomea x Rugosa**. A hybrid between two fine species, this has semi-double cerise-pink blooms. They are fragrant and pass on to round, medium-sized orange fruit. As you would expect, the foliage is bright green and resembles both parents.

Clinophylla (1816). Closely related to *R. bracteata*. Its large, white, single blooms are frequently used in religious ceremonies. Very fertile and produces seed freely. Native to a specific area in India, it has been known as *R. involucrata*.

Damascena. Here is a species that came to me by way of Israel. Reputed to be very near the true species, it has quite large, bright-pink, double blooms which are very fragrant. I understand that this rose is naturalised round some of the Middle Eastern countries.

▼ **Davidii Elongata Rosea**. A very pretty deep-pink form of the parent. The blooms are single, with only five petals, in lovely shades of bright, deep cerise-pink. The large fruit are similar to the parent's.

► **Dumalis Adenophora**. There seem to be many hybrids from *R. dumalis*. The type is widespread in much of western Asia and Europe. No doubt many of the forms recognised by some authorities are close to the parent. Foliage is greyish-green, with large fruit.

Ecae Helen Knight (1966). There is no doubt that this comparatively new hybrid from *R. ecae* will be popular. It has attractive, fern-like foliage and deep yellow, small, cupped flowers which are produced very freely. One flowering season.

Filipes Treasure Trove (1979). A lovely new form which is from 'Filipes Kiftsgate' and 'Buff Beauty'. Deliciously fragrant, it has large sprays of cupped, 3 cm flowers, warm apricot in colour. Very strong growth which will reach at least 9–10 metres.

▼ **Gallica**. We can never be sure that we really have specimens of these very old species. This very old form has single, bright pink blooms which appear freely on a smallish, compact plant. Nice fragrance.

A Celebration of Old Roses

▲ **Gallica x Rugosa**. This unusual hybrid has very pretty semi-double, open flowers, about 8 cm across, bright pink or light red, with a white centre. The gallica blood in this union must be strongest, as the foliage resembles the gallicas well.
Giraldii (1897). A native of central China, this rose is considered by some to be rather ordinary. The small single blooms are pink, the foliage a greyish-green. Lovely autumn foliage.
▶ **Iberica**. This species is not known in many quarters but is familiar enough in Iran and surrounding countries. The source of the plant pictured is a monastery garden in the Khandavu Pass. Medium-sized, single, white blooms.

Lutescens Erecta. There is a distinct possibility that this rose was introduced from Iceland. It seems to be marginally different from *R. spinosissima hispida*, with which it is often confused. Sulphur-yellow flowers appear on a plant up to 2 metres. Plentiful small prickles.

▶ **Macrantha Harry Maasz** (1939). Another very good hybrid to add to those from *R. macrantha*. It has a low-growing or spreading habit, and lovely deep-green foliage. The blooms are a little more than single, large, cupped, coloured cerise-crimson with a white centre.

Macrantha Ma Surprise (1872). There are several lovely hybrids from *R. macrantha*, and this is one you do not see very often. It has large blooms which are nicely double, white with pale salmon-pink shadings. Fragrant.

Macrophylla Château de Vaire (1934). A once-flowering hybrid from the type. It has nicely cupped, deep-crimson

double blooms and the healthy plant has deep bronzy foliage and grows up to 2 metres high.

Macrophylla Master Hugh (1966). Apparently this hybrid is a natural cross found in the wild. It grows to 3 metres or so and has quite large, red-flushed flowers followed by very large fruit. Makes a fine, free-standing plant for privacy or shelter.

▼ **Micrugosa Deep Pink**. Raised by Seizo Suzuki of Japan, this recent hybrid has all the attributes of the parent except that the large, single flower is a very pretty bright carmine-pink. Probably it grows taller as well.

▲ **Mollis**. Large, deep-pink
blooms sit nicely among
growth which is purplish in
colour. Because of its greyish-
green foliage, compact,
rounded habit and attractive
fruit, this species has become a
popular garden plant.

▶ **Moschata Narrow Water**.
Reputed to be a hybrid from
R. moschata nastarana, but
some say this is doubtful. I
must say that my plants bear a
very strong resemblance to it.
The small to medium flowers
appear in clusters. They are
pink and salmon-pink in the
bud, opening to blush-pink and
white — altogether a very
pretty combination.

◀ **Mulliganii**. A native of
western China, this is one of
the largest-growing members of
the family. It bears small,
single, white flowers in large
clusters, and the healthy,
vigorous plant can reach 8
metres or more. Small, orange-
red fruit. It is considered by
some to be the same as
R. longicuspis (below), but by
others to be different.

▼ **Multiflora Nana**. A pleasant
little rose, sometimes called the
'Engineer's Rose'. It is, as the
name implies, a dwarf form of
R. multiflora except that it has
the ability to flower again in
the late summer. Believed to be
one of the parents of the first
polyantha, 'Paquerette'.

Omeiensis Pteracantha Lutea. It seems that this lovely rose has been hidden away from us almost intentionally. The growth, leaves and thorns are very similar to the type, but the flowers, of course, are deep yellow. A real acquisition.

◄ **Oreophila**. This species has an affinity with *R. durandii* and *R. spaldingii*, and all three are considered to be forms of *R. nutkana*. It is possible that these relatives are forms of the one brought about by natural hybridising and climatic conditions. Small, single, pink blossoms; round red fruit.

▼ **Persica Euphrates** (1986). Jack Harkness, in his fascinating work with *R. persica*, has released three hybrids from his programme. This unusual rose has reddish-salmon, single flowers with wine-purple blotches in the throat. Once-flowering. Grows less than 1 metre high.

▲ **Persica Nigel Hawthorne** (1988). This, too, comes from the work Harkness has done with *R. persica*. (I have not seen this hybrid but understand it to be multicoloured and double.) I know that Nigel Hawthorne is extremely pleased with it, because he said so at the opening of the Festival of the Rose at St Albans in July 1988.

▼ **Persica Tigris** (1985). The first of the trio introduced by Jack Harkness, this is another *R. persica* hybrid. A rather beautiful and unusual rose, it has small yellow rosettes bearing the typical scarlet marking at the base of the petals.

▲ **Pomifera x Pendulina**. It could be said that this is a hybrid between *R. villosa* and *R. alpina*, which are synonyms for the species names above. This hybrid has single, pale pink flowers which are followed by bright orange, rounded fruit.

▼ **Rousseauiorum**. I doubt that this species will be known by many. It came to me by way of an exchange seed programme between botanical gardens around the world. An upright, healthy plant which grows to about 1.5 metres. The flowers are single, about 5 cm across, in the nicest shade of lilac-pink.

Rubrifolia Flora Plena. We are all aware of the beautiful *R. rubrifolia* and its uses in gardens, landscaping and utility planting. This is a double-flowered form of it, probably a hybrid. Small flowers, light red in colour.

Rubrifolia Sir Cedric Morris (1979). The flowers of this recent hybrid are single, small and white and adorn a very vigorous plant in huge clusters. It is nicely fragrant and the foliage is purplish when young and greyish when mature. Can easily grow to 9 or more metres.

▶ **Rugosa x Carolina**. An unusual hybrid in that the parents come from two worlds, *R. rugosa* from Japan and *R. carolina* from North America. The large, single, cerise-pink blooms with yellow stamens are very similar to the rugosas, and the foliage resembles the latter parent.

▼ **Rugotida**. Apparently this fine rose is a hybrid between *R. rugosa* and *R. nitida* and, as you would expect, has some attributes from both. It has medium-sized, cerise-pink blooms and large, rounded, rugosa-like fruit on a compact plant.

▼ **Sherardii** (1933). Two metres high and wide, with plenty of woody growth and bluish-green foliage, this rose has pink blooms and large fruit. It is native over a large area of northern and central Europe.

Spinosissima Robbie Burns (1985). Although this hybrid is quite new, it is old in its concept. It grows to over 1 metre high and has the usual prickly growth and ferny foliage of the family. It differs in that it has large single flowers, white at the centre with soft pink towards the edges.

► **Tuschetica** (1945). Although only introduced in recent years, no doubt this rose has existed in the wild for centuries. Its natural habitat in the USSR is the Daghestan mountain area. Pale- to medium-pink blooms and healthy bright green foliage.

▼ **Woodsii Ultramontana**. This is a very nice form of *R. woodsii* with bright cerise-pink, single, medium-sized blooms. The plant grows to about 2 metres high, and the flowers appear very freely, followed by a fine crop of rounded fruit.

Anacréon

Gallicas and their Hybrids

Although this family has been dealt with in a brief manner in my two earlier volumes, it seems appropriate and necessary to mention now a few more interesting facts. As *R. gallica* historically is one of the oldest families, it is important to realise its distribution over a wide area of Europe and the Middle East was due in part to Nature and in part to Man. During the heady days of the conquests by the Roman and Greek armies, roses were looked upon as important prizes of war. In fact, the conquering forces often had attached to them herbalists and physicians whose prime objective was to discover new and useful roses.

R. gallica is mainly found in countries that were formerly part of the tremendous empire of the Romans, and particularly in the thousands of monasteries later established by the Benedictine order. Because this rose had proven medicinal and perfume properties, there was never any doubt about its popularity and survival. It seems to be accepted that when the Moors invaded Spain in the early part of the eighth century, they took this rose with them, and consequently it moved on to the northern shores of the African continent, although it could just as easily have reached these areas from the opposite direction. It seems certain that *R. gallica* made its way to England some time before the twelfth century. An observant monk attached to St Mary's Abbey in York wrote in 1368: 'The red rose is ye badge of England and hath grown in this countrye for as long as ye mynde of man goeth.'

While examining some history and varieties of the French rose, it seems right to draw readers' attention again to the outstanding rose garden of Le Parc de Bagatelle in Paris.

From the visitor's point of view, it is well placed in the Bois de Boulogne, a huge green area near the centre of the city. The rose garden is easy of access and will well repay any effort it may take to reach it. ∎

▲ **Abailard** (1845). Robert, the French raiser, has been responsible for some fine roses and this striped hybrid is one of them. The flowers are quite double, of average size and light pink in colour with deep pink stripes.

Ambroise Paré (1846). It seems Vibert has had a hand in the raising of varieties in all the old families. This one from him has

rosette-shaped blooms of deep purplish-crimson. They are of medium size and double.

Anacréon (1836). A medium-to-tall grower from Vibert, with medium-sized, very double blooms which are light purplish-red and fragrant.

Aramis (1845). Believe it or not, this is another lovely hybrid from Vibert. It has white blooms with a light pink stripe. Of course, it is double, and fragrant.

Beauté de la Malmaison. Deep red blooms with purplish shadings which look very attractive on a healthy plant. The flowers are medium in size and fragrant. Raiser unknown.

A Celebration of Old Roses

▲ **Belle Sans Flatterie** (1820). This rose was considered to be very special in its day. It was raised by Godefroy and has rather nice medium-sized, mauvish-pink blooms, with a little late flowering.

▲ **Esther** (1849). Vibert is the introducer of yet another good rose with this pink, double variety which has a purplish stripe. It is fragrant and medium sized and sometimes called 'Grande Esther'.
▼ **Eucharis** (1815). A very old hybrid raised by Descemet which has light pink blooms that are large and double. Fragrant and vigorous.

▲ **Eveline**. Nothing is known about this rose's origins, but it is a fine one nonetheless. Bright pink, double, fragrant flowers.
▼ **Francois Foucquier**. There are a number of roses named after the various members of the Foucquier family. This hybrid has carmine-pink double blooms of good substance.
Général Moreau (1870). The Moreau family also have many roses named after them. This variety has a medium-sized bloom which is double, fragrant and mauvish-pink.

▲ **Gloriette**. Another old hybrid from an unknown raiser. It has blush-pink double flowers, freely produced in one flowering and, like quite a few in this group, sets nice fruit.

Helvetia. It seems incredible that there should be five roses with this name. All are in different families. This hybrid gallica is crimson with mauvish shadings.

Hypathia. A fine rose of unknown parentage. The double flowers appear on a healthy plant. They are medium-pink with a deeper pink centre and have a nice scent.

Jeannette (1815). Raised by Descemet, this hybrid is a strong and healthy grower with fragrant, double, red blooms of average size.

Josephine Parmentier (1840). Parmentier was responsible for many excellent roses and this is one of them. Of medium size, it is double and a pleasant shade of pink.

Juanita (1855). Large pink and white blooms, double and fragrant, are plentifully produced on a compact plant.

Ledonneau le Blanc. A little known variety which has blooms about 8 cm across, set nicely in deeper green foliage. They are large, double and white-shaded-pink in colour.

Mme Ville. Medium-sized, well shaped blooms of bright carmine-pink adorn an upright plant. Fragrant. Raiser unknown.

▼ **Madelon Friquet** (1830). Very double large flowers are the hallmark of this fine rose, and again Vibert is the introducer. The pink to light red blooms are fragrant and freely produced.

◄ **Manteau Royal** (1810). An excellent rose raised by Descemet. The nicely shaped blooms are double and of medium size, and are a bright red with fiery purple shadings. Descemet was a close friend of Vibert, and we should always be reminded that it was Vibert who very hurriedly removed tens of thousands of rose seedlings from Descemet's rose fields to his own nurseries, so that they would not be destroyed by the armies opposing Napoleon as they advanced on Paris in 1815. Perhaps some of the roses listed here were among those rescued at that time. This incident shows the friendship which has always seemed to exist among rose lovers and rose-growers all over the world, even to the present day.

◄ **Marie Antoinette** (1825). Tall-growing and healthy, this hybrid, again from Vibert, has purplish-pink, large, double blooms. In 1770 the people of the city of Provins were advised that Marie Antoinette would stop overnight under their care. They prepared a bed of rose petals for her on her way to marry the Dauphin, later to become Louis XVI.

▼ **Mazzeppa** (1848). There are a number of extremely interesting roses in this group, and if many of them survive, no doubt they will be appreciated. Double, pink, fragrant blooms on a healthy plant.

► **Président Dutailly** (1888). It is unusual for a member of the gallica family to have late flowers, but this hybrid does. It was raised by Dubreuil and has deep pink blooms with purplish shades at times, large, double and fragrant.

Pucelle de Lille (1860). Deep pink, large, double flowers grace an upright plant. Raised by Miellez, this hybrid used to be quite popular at one time.

Royal Marbré (1851). The French raisers Moreau and Robert are responsible for the introduction of this old-time favourite. It is a tall grower and has very double medium-sized flowers which are fragrant and light red to pink in colour.

Triomphe de Flore (1830). Nicely scented very double blooms appear on a tallish-growing plant. This variety was raised by Prévost and has light-pink blooms.

Turenne (1846). Medium-to-large double blooms of bright red with deepish-pink shades. They are scented and freely produced. Raised by Vibert.

► **Valence Dubois** (1880). A lovely hybrid of medium growth, raised by Fontaine. The blooms are of average size, double, fragrant and pink.

▼ **Victor Parmentier.** Apparently this attractive hybrid was found in the Roseraie de l'Hay, but the parentage and raiser are unknown. Its light red, fragrant blooms are medium sized and double.

► **Ville de Toulouse** (1876). Introduced by Brassac, this rose grows to a medium height. Its well shaped double blooms are pink and fragrant and it has healthy foliage.

Zoe (1840). A vigorous grower which has very double blooms, pink, fragrant and prolific, this rose was raised by Miellez.

Mme Lambert

Damasks and their Hybrids

There is no doubt that this family is one of the oldest on record, but unfortunately, as with the other old families, there are no clear proofs of its history. Many assumptions have been made, and if you took a little from all the known theories and put them together, the following could be the result.

Probably *R. damascena* came through the Middle East from unknown places further east. Its spread around the Mediterranean countries could be attributed to the Phoenicians or the Greeks, or both. The Romans had a hand in the saga and it eventually reached the west of Europe.

The family's greatest attribute seems to be in its use during the process of the distillation of attar of roses. Although this function has been going on for hundreds of years, there have been many modern programmes as well. One of the countries involved is the Soviet Union, whose production of attar of roses has now apparently become greater than that of Bulgaria, according to S. G. Saakov. He says Krasnodar is the research centre for the institute which deals with the scientific work of the projects. It is documented that the main centres for attar in the USSR are in the Crimea, where 1100 hectares (2718 acres) are planted, in the Moldavian Republic, which has 680 hectares (1680 acres), and in the Krasnodar area of the Caucasus, which has 800 hectares (1977 acres). The roses which are used mostly are the 'Red Crimean Rose' and the 'Red Kazanlik Rose'. The former appears to be a form from *R. gallica* while the latter is a form of *R. damascena trigintipetala*. From these two, several hybrids have been developed, and among the best of them are 'Nowinka', 'Piomerka' and 'Kooperatorka'.

The town of Grasse in the south of France seems to be the base for the French production of attar, and in Morocco the districts of Tedders, Maasis, Berkan and Marrakesh are responsible for that country's output of the valuable liquid. In India, Ghazipur, Poona and Bangalore have large plantings for this purpose, although it seems that most of this country's production is now jeopardised because of lack of technical progress. ∎

Adonis (1814). A fine rose with a fine name. Raised by Descemet, it has freely produced blooms of pink and blush-pink, double and quite large.

Angèle. It is not known where this excellent member of the family originated, but its large and very double flowers are quite distinctive. It is a pleasant light cerise-pink.

▼ **Babette**. Here, too, is a good rose about which we have no record of the raiser. The blush-to-white blooms are medium sized, double and appear quite freely on a tall plant.

► **Belisar** (1857). Again of unknown origin, but this does not mean that this rose is not worthy of the family. The flowers are double, of average size and blush-pink.

Belle Auguste. A lovely old damask with no known raiser. The light purplish-pink flowers are nicely double and reasonably large.

Christophe Colombe (1854). For a damask, this hybrid is fairly strong in colour, having larger, very double purplish blooms with an amaranth centre. Fragrant. Raised by Robert.

Claire. Bright pink blooms with lighter white and pale pink at the edges. They are well scented, large and double.

Dame Blanche. The large blooms are double and quite beautiful. They are freely produced, in one season of course, and of the purest white.

Divinité (1835). Prévost was the raiser of this lovely old variety. Sometimes it is called 'Bellefleur'. Deep pink flowers which are blush-pink in the centre and medium sized.

▲ **Duc de Chartres** (1820). Light pink, medium-sized flowers adorn a healthy plant. It is nicely fragrant and was raised by Godefroy.

Mme Carré. Blush-white, double blooms are profusely produced on a compact plant. A healthy grower, its origins are unknown.

Mme Lambert. The light pink flowers of this very old and little known variety are medium sized and double. They appear in profusion on a vigorous plant.

◄ **Mme Stolz**. This hybrid with creamy-white flowers appears to have been raised in England. The large, double flowers appear among light-green foliage.

Mme Tressant (1822). Most of the roses listed in this group are very old; this one, raised by Prèvost, has blush-white double blooms, medium to large and fragrant.

Marguerite de Flandre. A pretty hybrid with parentage and raiser unknown. It has nicely formed flowers which are double and fragrant. They are flesh-pink and plentiful.

Monstrueuse. Several roses carry this name and it can apply to either the foliage or the flowers. This hybrid has bright pink, unusually shaped blooms.

Noëmie (1845). Deep pink blooms which have a deeper fleck in them. They are fragrant, double and plentiful on a strong-growing plant. A Vibert production.

Olympe (1843). Vibert, a prolific raiser of roses, also produced this fine rose. Its well shaped blooms are cerise-pink and mauve. Double, medium-sized flowers.

Panachée (1820). There are not many striped roses in the damask family and this is one of them. Raised by Godefroy, the double white flowers have a light mauve stripe.

Pénélope (1818). Contrary to most opinion, there are many roses with the same name. In this case we have a gallica, a bourbon, a hybrid musk and a

Eudoxia. The lovely blooms of this very old variety are pink and mauvish-pink, fragrant, large and double. Raiser unknown.

◄ **Général Foy** (1825). Another very old hybrid, this time raised by Boutigny. The abundant, medium-sized, fragrant, double blossoms are deep pink with light red shades.

Henri IV. Raised by Trébucien, this too is an old hybrid. It has exceptionally large flowers which are, of course, double and fragrant. The colour is purplish-red.

◄ **Ismène** (1845). There is also a noisette and moss rose with this name. Another hybrid from that prolific producer of roses, Vibert, 'Ismène' has large, double, fragrant, blush-white blooms.

La Négresse (1842). There is some confusion as to whether Vibert or Robert raised this variety. The deep wine-red blooms are medium sized, double and fragrant.

damask all known as
'Pénélope'. This damask has
large, very double blooms of
light maroon-purple.

On the subject of different
roses bearing the same name, I
cannot for the life of me
understand why the hybridists
of today quite often adopt a
name for their particular rose
which has been used at least
once before, and sometimes
twice or more. It is
incomprehensible to me that
they should want to make use
of a name which someone else
has chosen. In doing so they
really only add to the
confusion. Perhaps I can
forgive those raisers of long
ago for their action — after all,
they did not have the benefit of
the records we now have access
to, and communications were
very primitive and slow to say
the least. Modern hybridists
have many advantages when it
comes to names for their
creations, yet sometimes they
choose to lapse into laziness
when they really could do
much better.

► **Périclès** (1830). Very double,
medium-sized blooms which
are freely produced on a
healthy plant. Vibert again was
the introducer, and this rose
has purplish-pink flowers.

Petite Agathe (1860). Small,
double flowers of mauvish-pink
are abundantly produced on a
compact plant. This hybrid was
raised by Baumann.

Pope. We have here a variety
with no known raiser. It has
very large, double blossoms
which are cerise-pink and
crimson in the centre. Fragrant.

Princesse du Portugal. There is
not a lot known about this
hybrid, whose raiser remains a
mystery. It has large pink
flowers, fragrant and well
formed.

Rose Préval (1825). Prévost
was the raiser of this rather
unusual rose. It has large, light
pink, very double flowers.

Different in that it can have
quite a few late blooms.

Rose Verhaux. Mauve-pink,
large, double flowers which are
very fragrant and quite
beautiful. Origins unknown.

► **Théone**. A very old variety
about which nothing seems to
be known. It has medium-
sized, fragrant, double blooms
of an even shade of pink.

Triomphe de Lille (1859).
Sometimes known as 'Bride of
Lille'. Vibert certainly was a
busy hybridist. This creation of
his has carmine-pink, middle-
sized blooms, double and
fragrant.

Triomphe de Rouen (1826).
Large, double blooms, lilac-
pink, nicely fragrant and
produced freely. This excellent
variety was raised by Lecomte.

Trois Mages (1823). Again an
old variety about which there is
precious little known. It has
pink, very double flowers of
medium size.

Valette. This beautiful member
of the group has well shaped,
double flowers of medium
pink, tending to pale at the
edges. Parentage and raiser
unknown.

Veturine (1842). Another grand
variety raised by Vibert. It has
light mauve-pink blooms which
are quite fragrant, very large
and nicely double.

Volumineuse. To complete this
group of mainly very old
damask roses, we have a
variety which is excellent and
yet little is known about it.
Double, fragrant pink.

Mme Hardy

Albas and their Relatives

Probably no one will believe that so many examples of this distinctive family still exist. I certainly did not until I saw most of those listed here present in the state rosarium at Sangerhausen in the German Democratic Republic. This treasure-house of old roses contains many hundreds of old favourites which are available through the usual process of importation and quarantine. One has to be very patient in carrying out this painstaking process, which sometimes results in a great degree of success and sometimes in none at all. The propagation of the roses themselves is quite complicated, but my first journey to Sangerhausen could be described as even more so.

It was general knowledge that tour parties wishing to visit East Germany did not have any real problems in doing so, but for a lone traveller wishing to visit a specific destination, I found that there was a different set of rules. Firstly, a visit to the legation in London saw me sent on to Berolina, the East German travel agency. Against other advice, I was told I had to go to Leipzig instead of Erfurt, which was infinitely closer to the rosarium. On arrival in Leipzig after a very long train journey, I had my passport taken from me and was told that Sangerhausen was off-limits to me. However, next morning the decision was reversed and I was on my way.

I arrived at Sangerhausen Railway Station and, because of circumstances beyond my control, had only about two hours to find the garden and catch the train under the terms of my visa. It was Good Friday, 1984, and the station was crowded so my chance of getting a taxi was slim, to say the least. I walked off down the hill, intending to find the rosarium on foot. A lone Russian, who was somewhat the worse for drink, got me a lift to the rosarium with a local resident. By now there was a little over an hour left before my train departed but the time was well used. My welcome at Sangerhausen more than made up for the travelling difficulties, and although we could not speak each other's language, we were able to communicate through the international medium of roses. ■

Alice (1830). A fine variety raised by the eminent French grower, Parmentier. It has double blooms of medium size which are white and blush-pink.
Ancelin. Here we have a hybrid of unknown origin which has attractive large blooms, very double, deep pink and quite fragrant.

Astrée. Blush-pink towards the outer petals and pink deeper down is the colour of this very double and very large-flowered hybrid. It is fragrant and vigorous.
Belle de Ségur (1935). There are three roses with this name — one centifolia and two albas. This hybrid was raised by Lelieur, the man responsible for 'Rose du Roi'. It has double, large blooms which are flesh-pink fading to white.
Belle Élise. An old hybrid of unknown origins. Again there are three roses with this name — one centifolia, one china and this one. The flowers are medium sized, nicely double and bright pink.
▼ **Belle Thérèse** (1835). Raised by Prévost, this is a fine member of the group. The light pink, large, double flowers are strongly scented.

Camille Bouland (1836). This too was raised by Prévost, who was responsible for many roses in the old families. The light-pink flowers, medium sized and double, are prolific.

Candide (1825). It seems impossible that there should be five roses with this name, but it is true. This one, a hybrid from Vibert, has white blooms with a pale salmon flush.

Celeste Blanche. Little is known of this rose's origins. Possibly it is a sport from 'Celestial'. The medium-sized, semi-double to double blooms are pure white and blush-pink in the bud.

Claudine (1823). Another fine rose from Vibert. Pure white, semi-double flowers appear on a typical alba-type plant.

Élise. This, too, is a rose about which very little is known. It has double, bright pink flowers which are fragrant and freely produced.

Enfant de France (1830). Sometimes called 'Beauté Tendre', again this is a Vibert production. It is blush-pink above and white below. Flowers are medium sized and double.

Fanny. This rose has medium-sized blooms which are double like so many others in the group. They are cerise-pink, inclined to pale lemon at the base.

Ferox. A pretty rose, but we do not know who is responsible for its creation. Flesh-pink and white, nicely shaped double flowers.

▼ **Gabrielle d'Estrée** (1819). Bearing white and blush-pink double flowers, this is one of the oldest hybrids in the group. It might belong to the damask family, but seems to me to be quite at home here. Raised by Vibert.

Henriette Campan (1855). The light mauvish-pink blooms make this hybrid a little different from most others in the group. Fragrant, double and of average size.

Lucrèce (1844). It seems the French raiser Vibert was most prolific when it came to albas, for this is another of his creations. It has very large blooms of blush-pink, double and fragrant.

Mme Audot (1845). This could be described as an excellent member of the group from Victor Verdier. Medium pink and flesh-pink blooms adorn a healthy plant.

Royale (1835). There seems to be some confusion over this variety as well. Another Vibert hybrid, it has large, blush-pink, double blooms, with the typical greyish-green foliage.
Sara. Small, double, pink flowers adorn a compact plant. They are fragrant and freely produced. Origin not known.
Superbe. This is truly a superb rose, with double, fragrant blooms of pure white. Again we have the typical greyish-green foliage and healthy, vigorous growth.
Surprise (1823). A lovely variety raised by Pailpré. Pink, fading to white at the edges, the blooms are double, fragrant and small to medium in size.
Vaucresson. Another very old variety about which little is known, It has well formed flowers of blush-pink which have a white base, very double and fragrant.
▼ Venus. Believe it or not, there are six roses which have this name, and each of their raisers probably thought theirs was the best. This one has double, white, fragrant blooms.

▲ Mme Hardy. Nothing seems to be known about this hybrid's origins. Not to be confused with the damask of the same name. This, too, is white and double. Fragrant.
Marie de Bourgoyne (1850). Again we have a fine rose from Vibert. Its blooms are pink with white marks or flecks, fragrant, large and very double.
Monica. In the collecting and studying of old roses I have found many with female names. Has medium-sized, double, pink blooms.
Persicafolia. White blooms with pale lemon or blush-pink in the throat. There is some confusion over this rose's origin and classification. The name 'Persicafolia' probably arises from the appearance of the foliage.
Placidie (1820). Semi-double, small, light pink flowers grace this compact-growing plant which was raised by Prévost.
Remarquable. Probably because of their age, there are quite a few roses in this group about which very little is known. As here, the date of introduction and the raiser's name is often missing. This variety has white, double flowers.
Rose du Matin (1835). There are some who believe this is the alba 'Chloris' and others who consider it is different. Medium-pink, double and fragrant.

Zénobie. To complete this group we have another fine rose from Vibert. The medium-sized, even pink blooms are nicely scented.

Horatius Cocles

Centifolias and their Hybrids

It seems the origins of this family will always be clouded in mystery, It is quite likely that centifolias were known over 2000 years ago. Many are the tales and theories about where they came from, none of which can be proved, of course. The best that can be offered is the approximate date of their arrival in certain countries. One thing is certain, as with the other old families discussed in this volume, there were a tremendous number of these old centifolias in existence at one time, and although a few have been popularised, there are a great number of them available in European gardens and not available elsewhere. The roses presented here lose nothing by comparison with those already known.

Whenever one's thoughts turn to the five oldest families and the species, the name of the famous man who painted these roses, Pierre-Joseph Redouté, automatically comes to mind. He was born in St Hubert, near Liège in Belgium, and spent much of his young days wandering through the Ardennes. To me this beautiful area of woods and rolling hills is a very serene and peaceful place, and perhaps this was to influence Pierre-Joseph more than he realised. During his long life he rubbed shoulders with royalty, aristocrats and statesmen as well as the common people, yet he never seemed to be out of his depth with any of them. He lived through turbulent times, to say the least; he suffered personal tragedy, and yet through all this he was able to produce the finest work, which really has not been equalled since.

Redouté was an honest, conscientious man of humble beginnings who seemed to have some form of inner peace which took him successfully through a long and eventful life. His rewards were many, though perhaps rather more material than monetary, and through it all he remained entirely devoted to his art. As well as being a master of botanical illustration, he was an author of some note. He received several honours from his adopted country, and when his time came finally, he was teaching a class at the Jardin des Plantes in Paris. A wonderful man, a remarkable talent and in every way a tremendous example to us all. ■

Black Boy (1958). Perhaps it is a little strange to commence this group with a recent hybrid from the house of Kordes. Nevertheless it is strongly scented and has deep crimson flowers of medium size which are quite double. A useful addition.

▼ **Centifolia Major** (1597). This is recognised by most as the original form. Pink, very double, very fragrant blooms. Also sometimes known as the 'Batavia Rose'.

Centifolia Minor Again, pink double blooms and strongly scented. Probably of great antiquity but as with Centifolia Major its origins are uncertain.
Comtesse de Ségur (1848). Verdier was the raiser of this fine hybrid. The medium-sized flowers are pink and blush-pink and are produced freely in season.

▲ **Crenata** (1810). A lovely old variety which has not been seen for some time. It was raised by André Dupont. The double flowers are bright pink and have unusual petal formation.
Decora. Probably a hybrid raised in France. The small pink blooms are very double and have a light scent. They appear prolifically on a tall-growing, healthy plant.

Duc de Brabant (1857). Another excellent variety raised, I believe, by an unknown French grower. The blooms are crimson, of average size and nicely double. They look well on a tall plant with deep green foliage.
► **Duchesse de Coutard**. Of unknown origin, this good representative of the class has well filled, cupped blooms of medium size, bright pink and fragrant.
◄ **Gaspard Monge** (1854). Light mauvish-red blooms adorn a healthy, vigorous plant. They are fragrant, of medium size and double. A hybrid raised by Robert.
Grande Centfeuille de Hollande (1840). A vigorous growing, healthy plant supports light pink, very double large flowers which are well scented. Raised by Prévost.

▲ **Horatius Cocles**. When delving into these old families it is always a matter of amazement how many beautiful roses there have been which to our eyes are little known. This one has double blooms, fragrant and medium pink.

Hulda. Another old variety which it is hoped will become better known. The flowers are deep purplish-crimson, of something like medium size and fairly double. 'Hulda' also has a nice scent.

▲ **Justine Ramet** (1845). A fine hybrid introduced by Vibert, who was a contemporary and friend of Redouté. This rose has lovely blooms of purplish-pink and deeper shadings at times.

Mousse de Meaux (1814). This is the mossy form of 'De Meaux' and probably should be grouped with that family. Like its parent, it is small and has pink and white, fragrant, rosette-like flowers. Introduced by Sweet.

Parkjuwel (1950). Nicely scented, this comparatively modern member of the group is deep red, double and of medium size. Raised by Kordes, it is vigorous and healthy.

Rose à Feuilles de Laitue (1815). Some authorities state that this variety, which was introduced by Duhamel, is similar to 'Bullata'. It has medium-pink, double blooms with a strong scent.

Röte Centifolie (1938). Probably because of its more recent introduction, this variety is a very good deep red with quite double flowers and a strong scent. Raised by Krause.

Stratosféra (1934). Nicely scented, medium-sized, very double blooms are produced freely on a tall plant. They are purplish-red and fragrant. Raised by Böhm.

Vierge de Clery (1888). White is not a common colour in the centifolias but here we have a pure white double bloom on a tallish plant. Introduced by Baron Veillard.

Wellington (1832). An early variety raised by Calvert. Bright pink, fragrant blooms quite freely appear on a plant with deep green foliage.

Césonie

Moss Roses and their Hybrids

There seems to be always some confusion about the moss rose family. Many people seem to think that any of the old roses are moss roses, and it is difficult to find out where this confusion started. It may be that at first glance many of the old beauties do not show their mossiness and from above they may all look alike. Maybe this is the reason why roses which do not have moss are sometimes called moss roses.

Like the other old families in this volume, there are many more members in this class than most people ever realised. Literally hundreds if not thousands were available during the height of the group's popularity. Again, we are indebted to those wonderful gardens in Europe for the preservation of these old moss roses. Many of them are now making their way from these treasure houses to the gardens of enthusiasts around the world. For me, not having been able to carry out a hybridising programme over the years, the importation and the propagation of the plants for sale is almost as thrilling.

Imagine a quarantine plot with something like 1000 plants from six countries in 250 varieties, just coming into flower for the first time. Our expectations are great, to say the least, because we have been able to locate information about what they should look like. Sometimes roses do not fit their description and of course there is disappointment, but usually most of them are correctly named. The rose hybridist must also feel this exhilaration when waiting for his creations to flower — waiting to see if this time the magic has worked, and the something special which he has awaited for years has at last arrived. It is a feeling that can only be experienced, described and appreciated by those who have carried out this work. ∎

Adèle Pavie (1850). A nicely scented rose to commence this group. The plant grows about 1 metre high and its attractive double flowers are blush-pink. A Vibert production.
Alcime (1861). This hybrid from Moreau and Robert has full, purplish-red flowers of medium size, freely produced.
Arthur Young (1863). Portemer was the hybridist who introduced this useful rose. It has deep purple, double blooms which contrast nicely with the plant's green foliage.
Céline Briant (1853). Produced by Robert, this excellent variety has well formed, double, pink flowers which are nicely fragrant. Of all the old moss roses, this one has some ability to put up late flowers.
Césonie (1860). This hybrid can also produce late flowers. They are cerise-pink with a carmine base, reasonably large and double. Produced by Moreau and Robert.

Circé (1856). William Paul was the raiser of this fine hybrid, which has pale pink and white flowers, medium in size and nicely double.
Clémence Robert (1864). Strongly scented pink and mauve blooms, double, large and freely produced. This hybrid can also have quite a nice lot of late flowers. Raised by Moreau and Robert.
Delille (1852). A fine old variety which offers a rewarding amount of late flowers. Raised by Robert, the rose has blooms of blush-pink with mauvish-pink shades, double and fragrant.
Ducis (1857). It seems Moreau and Robert raised many varieties during this heady period of the moss rose's popularity. The medium-sized double blooms are coloured light pink and mauve.
▼ **Etna** (1845). Here we have another fine moss rose raised by Vibert. The very double blooms are large and fragrant. Coloured carmine-purple, they have bronzy shades at times.

A Celebration of Old Roses

Fontaine (1852). Pink with deep pink shading is the colour of this once-popular member of the family. It has largish, double blooms, produced freely. Raised by Robert.

▼ **Hortense Vernet** (1861). Another Moreau and Robert production, this moss rose also has the ability to have late flowers. The double flowers, which have a good scent, are white and pale pink.

Indiana (1845). This rose with an American name is from the French grower, Vibert. Blooms are double, medium sized and a nice shade of bright pink.

Ismène (1854). Robert, a prolific producer of roses, is responsible for this fine rose, once in popular demand. Blush-pink blooms with pale mauve-pink in the centre.

Jacquinot. Pretty pink and white blooms are set in healthy, light green foliage. They are fragrant, medium sized and nicely double.

Jean Bodin (1847). Tall growing for a member of this group, this hybrid from Vibert has double pink flowers in profusion in season.

John Fraser (1862). A useful rose from Granger, which will have a reasonable amount of late flowers. The double blooms are bright red and deep carmine.

Joséphine. A pink, very old member of this group. Little known, but beautiful just the same.

Julie de Mersan (1854). One of the old striped varieties, this hybrid was raised by Thomas. The blooms are of average size and double, coloured deep pink with white stripes.

Mme Charles Salleron (1868). Another lovely old rose, this time introduced by Fontaine. Large and double, the blooms of carmine and red appear freely.

Mme Landeau (1875). The deep red flowers with thin white stripes are double and medium sized. They have the ability to appear again later. A useful rose from Moreau and Robert.

Mme Platz (1865). Moreau and Robert produced this fine rose too. It has a strong fragrance and the double blooms are a nice shade of pink.

Mme Soupert (1851). Here we have a hybrid which is remontant and also raised by Moreau and Robert. The red blooms are plentiful and appear on a compact plant which grows to about 1 metre.

Ninette (1857). The flowers of this hybrid are of medium size, nicely double and medium red in colour. Another creation of Moreau and Robert.

Oscar Leclerc (1853). Double blooms of deep red with lemon and lilac centre are the features of this pretty rose from Robert. A nice fragrance, too.

▲ **Parmentier** (1851). Another useful hybrid from Robert. Its deep pink blooms are reasonably large and quite double. They appear on a compact plant just over 1 metre high.

Pourpre du Luxembourg (1848). The semi-double, medium-sized blooms of this hybrid are deep purple with carmine shadings. Raised by Hardy.

▼ **Précoce** (1843). Vibert raised this good hybrid with double pink blooms which can be light red at times. They are fragrant and the plant is of medium height.

► **Princess Alice** (1853). The vigorous growth of this rose raised by A. Paul supports very good flowers which are deep pink, large and double.

Robert Fortune (1853). I wonder if Robert, the French hybridist, had his tongue in his cheek when he named this rose. The double flowers are lilac-mauve with deep violet stripes.

Soeur Marthe (1848). Another hybrid raised by Vibert. Follows the mould of most in this group with its large double blooms, which appear nicely on a tall-growing plant.

Unique (1852). Rosette-shaped flowers of cerise-purple make this variety from Robert rather different. The double blooms sometimes have white shadings.

Valide (1857). Rosy-carmine double flowers grace this hybrid which is from Moreau and Robert. Once more we have a variety which has quite a nice late flowering.

▲ **William Grow** (1859). Laffay, not to be outdone, joins our list with this lovely old rose. The double flowers are fragrant and deepish purple at first, lightening as they age.

Zaire (1849). Vibert raised this last variety in our group. It grows to something over 1 metre high and has deep pink, well filled flowers which are fragrant.

Buffon

Portlands and their Hybrids

It is well recorded that although this family probably originated from the damasks, and most likely the autumn-flowering ones at that, many of the 150 or so which made up the class did not possess the ability to flower again later. However, I must say that of the thirty or more varieties I have had dealings with, this does not seem to be true.

Again, I must disagree with those who say that the Portland family is of little worth. I would liken this to rejecting a person simply because one did not see eye to eye with that person. What I think happens in this case is that the Portlands as a whole are compared with all the roses which have appeared right up to the present day, and of course they do have some shortcomings. But what one has to do to appreciate the family is to shut out of one's mind those that have come after, and see and study this family in its own time and in its own right.

Another subject which I think we should look at very carefully is the names of all the old roses and our treatment of, or rather our resistance to, them. We should open our minds and vision to the fact that a high percentage of all the old roses originated in Western Europe and naturally the names given them would appear foreign to us. Remember that for gardeners in France, Denmark, Germany or any other countries nearby, where the population is huge and the roses present in their thousands, it is not strange to have a rose named in their own language. It is we who are in the minority and we who should accept and use the names given to these creations of extreme beauty. ■

Buffon (1836). An upright plant of unknown origin which has medium-sized, very double blooms of bright pink with a red base. They are fragrant and typically sit well into the foliage.
Capitaine Renard (1843). Again a hybrid of unknown origin, but one of distinct beauty nevertheless. It has blush-pink, double blooms with white shading. Nice healthy, bright green foliage sets off the blooms very well.
Casimir Delavigne (1851). Raised by Robert, who was a prolific producer of hybrids about this time. The flowers are lilac-pink, large, quite double and, like most of the family, fragrant.

Céline Bourdier (1851). In the same year Robert also produced this variety. It has purplish-red, large blooms, freely produced on an upright, healthy plant.
Desdemona (1841). This is a pretty little rose which has long since been passed over for something supposedly better. It was raised by Robert and has small, purplish, double flowers.
Henriette Boulogne (1845). Strongly scented, this large-flowered variety is an attractive rose whose blush-pink blooms are produced freely.
▼ **Jules Lesourd** (1863). Moreau and Robert were busy during the time that the Portlands were popular. This hybrid of theirs has double, light red blooms.

◄ **Palmyre** (1817). This famous old hybrid also had a good measure of popularity in its day. Raised by Vibert. The blooms are double, large and of medium-bright pink.

Portland Blanche (1835). A very pretty rose which is medium sized and double with a nice scent. Raised by Vibert, it is white and blush-pink in the bud.

Portland Pourpre (1830). This rose's light mauvish-purple, semi-double small flowers have a cerise-pink base. It is a hybrid raised by Prévost and has a nice scent.

Prince de Galles. Small, compact growth with flowers that are double, scented and light red in colour, or occasionally mauvish-pink.

La Moderne. Also referred to as a 'fleurs doubles', this very old variety is double, of medium mauvish-pink in colour. It is nice to see that old roses like this one are still surviving.

Lesueur (1853). Medium-sized blooms of light red and mauve-pink are borne on a typical rounded plant. They are large, double and fragrant.

► **Mme Souveton** (1874). A little different from the usual hybrids in this group, this rose is semi-double. Pink and white in colour, it is not very tall-growing and was raised by Pernet.

Marie Robert (1850). Another variety which seems to have passed into oblivion. For a short space of time at least it was much admired. Raised by Moreau and Robert, it is mauvish-pink and double.

Mathilde Jesse (1847). This fine rose is not well known. It is a compact grower and the blooms sit nicely among the bright green foliage. They are medium to large, and bright red in colour.

▲ **Robert Perpétual** (1856). An extremely pretty rose which I have come to appreciate very much. The colour is a combination of mauvish-pink and at times deeper shades. The flowers are large, quite double and freely produced.

Sylvia (1835). This, too, was raised by Vibert and is cerise-pink at the edges, fading to a lighter colour at the base of the petals. The blooms are double, nicely shaped and fragrant.

Reynolds Hole

Bourbons and their Hybrids

Contrary to many people's opinion, quite a number of the early bourbon roses were, in the main, summer-flowering also. Probably it was the hybrids raised later which had some remontancy bred into them. There are, of course, quite a few families mixed up in their parentages and, as you would expect, many well known hybridisers were involved in their creation. Not the least of these was Pierre Guillot.

Although early methods of raising roses were fairly primitive by modern standards, in the middle of the nineteenth century that was no barrier to the house of Guillot producing some very fine roses. As with most early hybridising establishments, success was not always forthcoming for Pierre Guillot. However, he was able to create a worthwhile base from which to develop. He had the handling of two important roses, 'Géant des Batailles', a hybrid perpetual, and 'Mme Bravy', a tea rose, although he did not raise them. Pierre's son, Jean-Baptiste, followed in his father's footsteps.

If for nothing else, Pierre will be remembered for collecting seed of *R. canina*, and others, and for growing his rootstocks from seedlings rather than from cuttings, which was the practice of the time. Eventually all rose-growers adopted this method. Jean-Baptiste is remembered for the introduction of the first hybrid tea, 'La France', and the first polyantha, 'Paquerette'.

For me, the name 'Guillot' has special significance. Although not connected with the Guillot family, having been raised by Charles Mallerin, 'Mme Henri Guillot' was one of the first roses I knew. It grew as a standard rose along the street from my home when I cycled to high school during World War Two. This rose was on the end of a row of five different roses in a garden surrounding a home of which I was always envious. The rose was a beautiful deep salmon-pink, with glossy green foliage, and it stood out like a beacon. Usually I would cycle on the footpath and this brought me closer to that lovely rose. Why did I ride on the footpath? In those days the street was just rough shingle but the footpath was asphalted. Although not aware of it at the time, I was already irrevocably hooked on roses. ∎

► **Amarante** (1859). This hybrid, introduced by Page, is quite distinctive. It has medium-sized flowers which are double, purplish-carmine and red in the centre. Sometimes it repeats. Fragrant.
Angèle Fontaine (1878). A fine rose with cerise-pink blooms. It has medium-sized, double flowers which are quite prolific on a healthy plant. Raised by Fontaine.

▼ **Catherine Guillot** (1861). Bred from 'Louise Odier', this beautiful hybrid is well scented and has purplish-pink blooms which are medium sized and very double. A Pierre Guillot production.

A Celebration of Old Roses

Comtesse de Rocquigny (1874). Vaurin raised this variety, which is not so well known these days. Tall growing, it has medium-sized, double flowers which are white and blush-pink.

De Lille. Large, very double blooms are the hallmark of this very good hybrid. The mauvish-pink flowers, perhaps because of their size, are not so prolific as on some other varieties.

Emotion (1862). Here is a fine rose which I feel has been underestimated. Raised by Guillot, it is light to medium pink, quite double and fragrant.

Le Roitelet (1869). Soupert was responsible for this attractive variety. It does not have very big flowers, in fact they are quite small. Being pink and double, they look well against the healthy, light green foliage.

Lorna Doone (1894). Cerise-pink and scarlet are the colours of this double, medium-sized flower. Strongly scented, it was a popular rose in its day. Introduced by William Paul.

◄ **Mme d'Enfert** (1904). The raiser of this variety, Vilin, is not well known, but that does not mean it is not a good rose. The large blooms are double and profuse on a medium-sized plant. They are white and light pink.

▲ **Euphémie** (1830). Bright pink, medium-sized, double blooms grace this upright plant with bright foliage. It is an old variety and an old favourite. Raised by Vibert.

► **Frau O. Plegg** (1909). This hybrid was raised by Nabonnand and is quite beautiful. Reminiscent of a David Austin English rose, it has medium-sized, double, deep crimson blooms which are strongly scented.

J. B. M. Camm (1900). Another excellent example of the family, this rose was raised by G. Paul. It has light pink flowers of medium to large size, very double and nicely scented.

▲ Mme Dubost (1890). Pernet joins the ranks of the bourbon raisers with this good rose of long ago. The blooms are very double, medium sized and coloured white and light pink.

Mme de Stella (1863). The house of Guillot produced many roses and this is another of their raising. Light pink, large, double blooms in profusion.

Mme Foureau. Possibly this hybrid should be listed as a noisette but some believe it belongs here. Medium-growing, the blooms are double, large and creamy-white.

Mme Jeannine Joubert (1877). Margottin raised many fine roses and this is one of them. Light red, double flowers appear abundantly on a plant about 1.5 metres high.

A Celebration of Old Roses

▲ **Mme Nobécourt** (1893). Moreau and Robert had quite a large hand in raising many of the early hybrids, including this tall-growing, strongly scented, very large flowering variety which has light pink blooms.

Mlle Claire Truffaut (1887). Not to be outdone by the other raisers of the time, Verdier joined the team with this fine hybrid which has light pink, large, double blooms appearing plentifully on a medium-sized plant.

Mlle Marie Dauvesse (1861). This variety also has large, light pink blooms which are double and appear profusely on a plant to about 1.5 metres. Raised by Vigneron, who also was responsible for many other roses.

▼ **Monsieur A. Meille** (1889). Another Moreau-and-Robert-raised rose, this is quite distinctive with its very large, double blooms of deep crimson. They are strongly scented and the plant is tall growing.

Monsieur Cordeau (1892). From the Moreau and Robert stable, this is a tall-growing plant supporting extremely fragrant, very large, double blooms of bright scarlet-crimson.

Président de la Rocheterie (1891). Good roses are not hard to find in this group. This is another excellent example. The double flowers are very big, crimson with a purple centre, and strongly fragrant. Raised by Vigneron.

Reynolds Hole (1862). A fine rose which was very popular in its day. The colour is pale creamy-salmon, deeper at times. Double, medium-sized blooms are freely produced on a medium-sized plant. Raised by Standish.

Sir Joseph Paxton (1852). Laffay produced this pinkish-

light red or deep pink blooms are large and double.

Souvenir de Victor Landeau (1890). It seems that Moreau and Robert were more active with the bourbons than with other families. Here we have a vigorous grower with very large double flowers of scarlet-crimson.

Souvenir du Lieutenant Bujon (1891). Nicely fragrant, the very large, double, light red blooms are freely produced on a tall plant. This variety was also raised by Moreau and Robert.

Souvenir d'un Frère (1850). Oger is the introducer of this hybrid. A vigorous grower, the plant freely produces medium-sized, double flowers of deepish purple-crimson, with crimson-carmine at the base.

red variety which is well scented. The large, double flowers are abundantly produced on a vigorous plant.

Souchet (1842). Purplish-red large blooms are prolific on a healthy plant. They are double and have a heavy fragrance. The plant grows to about 1.5 metres. A Souchet hybrid.

Souvenir d'Anselme (1800). This French-raised variety is perhaps little known but nevertheless quite pretty. The

▲ **Victoire Fontaine** (1882). A seedling from 'Catherine Guillot', this was raised by Fontaine. The pink flowers have a purplish-pink base. They are medium sized and double.

Zigeunerblut (1890). This hybrid from Geschwind has some *R. alpina* blood in it, and because of this the wood is almost thornless. The large, double blooms, which reflex nicely, are deep cerise-purple.

Boursault Roses

It has been written by some critics that this family is of little import and the members of it never reached great heights. This may be true, but it is no real justification for discarding them out of hand. They were created and they existed, and in their own time they were beautiful. In several ways they also helped to form the families that came later. The boursaults were quite difficult to hybridise and it seems that only Vilmorin and Laffay were at all successful.

Monsieur Boursault, the man after whom this group was named, was an amateur rosarian who was in the happy situation of having quite a large rose garden and who was able to make extensive tours for study and relaxation. His knowledge and experience were much sought after by the breeders of the day and once his approval was given to a new seedling, it was like a royal stamp of approval and of course almost guaranteed a measure of success. Many attempts were made by his friends to name a rose after him but he always refused his permission until this family came along. On seeing the first of these new hybrids he was so enthusiastic that he gave approval for his name to be used.

The hybrids which follow add a few more to the list of this not very large family. It is regrettable that our visit to the gardens in Denmark and the two Germanys, although calculated to be at the best flowering time for the old families, was actually too late. Because of this I have no pictures of the varieties that follow. ∎

Belle Sultane (1800). This hybrid is also known under the name 'Maheca'. We saw the rose in Sangerhausen. It has purplish-violet blooms which are large and nicely double. Like others in the family, it is tall growing.

Drummond's Thornless. Little known, this variety has semi-double flowers of pinkish-carmine. As the name implies, the wood is quite thornless. Introduced by Drummond.

L'Orléanaise (1899). The parentage of this fine member is given as 'Mme Sancy de Parabere' x *R. florida*. The flowers are very large, very double and have pink, blush-pink and white in them. The plant grows to 2 metres or so and is quite hardy.

Laevis. Large, single flowers of purplish-red appear along the arching branches on this unique variety. Also known as 'Glabra' and 'Vulgaris'.

Turbinata. An old rose which seems to be loosely related to this family. Semi-double, lightly fragrant, purplish-pink. Grows to 2 metres. Also may be known as 'Venusta'. Attractive fruit.

Variegata. Lightly double blooms of lilac-pink with an occasional darker stripe. Tall growing, with few thorns.

Albert Hoffman plaque, Sangerhausen state rosarium

L'Admiration

Chinas and their Hybrids

Again, a fine representative collection of roses is present in this group. Most of what has been said about the other families in this volume also applies to the china roses. There are many more varieties existing than we ever thought possible, and they were created by many of the people who were working in the other groups as well.

One of these was Luther Burbank, of Santa Rosa, California. There are many stories relating to his work late last century and as with all people who appear to be different in a greater or lesser way, he had many critics. Nevertheless, we really must accept that he was 'a wizard with plants' and did create many new varieties in quite different branches of the plant kingdom. The Americans have a saying that 'a weed is a plant that has not got a good press agent', and it may be that some of Burbank's introductions were rather ordinary, but with his excellent advertising and promotional efforts he was able to sell some of his hybrids for very large sums of money.

We are concerned, of course, only with his work with roses, and he did introduce quite a group of them. We do not know if they were bred intentionally or if they were just chance seedlings, for he did not keep any records of his work. In fact, he is on record as saying that 'if one were to attempt to trace their multiple ancestry, there would be little time left for any other experiments'.

Among numerous rose varieties which he raised, best known was probably 'Burbank', said to be bred from 'Bon Silene' and a seedling from 'Hermosa'. W. Atlee Burpee is reputed to have paid $US500 for this rose. Whatever criticisms have been made

about the life and times of Luther Burbank, no one could ever say that he was shy when it came to putting a price on one of his productions. ■

► **Alice Hamilton** (1904). A lovely little rose to start this group, and typical of the family. Semi-double, light pink and deep pink blooms are freely produced on a small-growing plant. It has a nice scent and was raised by Nabonnand.

▼ **Alice Hoffman** (1897). Not unlike the previous rose, but of a more even pink colour and with more petals. Healthy growth on a small plant supports a plentiful crop of flowers. Albert Hoffman was the raiser.

I saw this rose during my first visit to Sangerhausen and felt that I had come across it before. This was not true but it was some time before I realised why I had this feeling. The following story may seem irreverent to some readers but I relate it to show how coincidences happen. Some years ago my wife and I were touring in and near Santa Barbara, California. Late in the day we called in to see our host's nephew, who happened

to run a funeral parlour, and inevitably we were taken through to inspect the place. We found it a most interesting experience. We came to a large room that resembled a chapel and, much to our surprise, at the front of this room there was a casket with the upper half propped open. Sitting upright in the casket, as if she were alive and watching the world go by, was a little, grey-haired old lady, and on the nearby plaque was the name 'Alice Hoffman'.

Bébé Fleuri (1906). This is a lovely little rose from Dubreuil. It has semi-double small flowers in clusters, pink with white in the middle. The plant only grows to about 40 cm, and it is an excellent little rose.

▲ **Burbank** (1900). Double, fragrant, light pink. It is said that Luther Burbank produced this rose specifically for bedding purposes. It was extremely free flowering and, when entered in the World's Fair in St Louis in 1904, it won the gold medal for the best bedding rose in the world — no mean feat even in those days.

Cramoisi Éblouissant. A variety which originated in Holland. Of typical china appearance, it has small, double, deep carmine-red blooms produced, as with all the family, very freely on a small, twiggy, healthy plant.

Darius (1827). An old hybrid produced by Laffay, this rose is not seen very often these days. Typically, it has small, double flowers on a small plant. They are a nice shade of violet-mauve.

James Sprunt (1858). This is a climbing sport of 'Cramoisi Supérieur' and is quite beautiful when established. The twiggy growth is slow to build up, but when it does the effect is very showy. Small, double, scarlet-crimson flowers in profusion.

► **Jean Bach-Sisley** (1899). Light pink, medium-sized, double flowers grace a small-growing, typically twiggy plant. They are strongly scented and produced abundantly. Raised by Dubreuil.

L'Admiration (1856). Robert is responsible for this fine single rose, pink and of medium size. The plant grows to about 1 metre and is a very pretty sight when laden with flowers.

Miralda (1830). This is the only striped china I have found so far. The blooms are very double and small. They are deep violet-crimson and have a red stripe. Introduced by Vibert.

Nubienne (1825). Deep red, almost burned red, in colour, these blooms are medium-sized double. The plant is rather tall growing for a member of this group. A hybrid from Laffay.

Old Blush Climbing. I first saw this rose growing about 10 metres up a tree in Palo Alto, California, some years ago. Obviously it is very vigorous and, like its bush parent, is never really without blooms. A very useful addition to the climbing family.

▼ **Pallida** (1843). A small grower, this useful rose is light

pink in colour, medium in flower size, double, with many blooms at one time, and nicely scented. It was raised by Feast.

Pompon de Paris Climbing. An exact replica of its parent except, of course, in its growth, this rose has small, double, pink flowers. It grows to about 1.5 metres and is useful for those small areas where a vigorous rose would soon get too big.

▼ **Pourpre** (1827). Deep purplish-red is the colour of this medium-sized, single rose. The blooms are produced profusely on a small-growing plant. Raised by Vibert.

Primrose Queen (1922). Of all the members of this group which I have become acquainted with, 'Arethusa' has been one of the most popular. Its fresh colour and sweet scent stand out. This variety is a colour sport from it and has blooms in shades of light yellow.

► **Richelieu** (1845). Purplish-pink, large, very double blooms are produced freely on a plant of medium height. This quite old hybrid was raised by Verdier.

▼ **Röte Hermosa** (1899). Not a colour sport of 'Hermosa' as you would perhaps think, but a cross between that rose and 'Reine Marie Henriette'. Nicely scented, the double flowers are deep reddish-carmine. Raised by Geissler.

▼ **Saint Prist de Breuze** (1838). A pretty little rose, typical of the family. Introduced by Desprez, it has lightly double blooms, deep carmine-pink on the outer petals and pink in the centre.

◄ **Santa Rosa** (1900). The parentage given for this hybrid from Burbank is the same as for the rose 'Burbank'. Similar in many ways to the former, but seems to have less petals. Light pink and fragrant.

▼ **Setina, Climbing Hermosa** (1879). Located by Henderson but introduced by Schwartz, this is a sport from the original. It is pleasing to have a climbing form, which of course has many more flowers than the bush form.

Triomphe de Laffay (1830). Laffay must have thought a lot of this rose to name it in this way. It has double, medium to large blooms, pink with white in colour. A grand rose to complete the group.

Mme Martignier

Noisettes and their Hybrids

We who collect and admire old roses in every shape and form tend to think that we have a reasonably good knowledge of them, but this really is not true. Perhaps I should explain. We know a great deal about those roses that we are familiar with, and we are inclined to think that that is the end of it. But what we do not realise is that there are countless more varieties in all of the families still existing, which are being grown, loved, and studied. Those of us who live in the so-called 'Western' countries really have the blinkers on when it comes to old roses.

While on the subject of East and West, I think it is about time we put these terms aside and simply spoke about countries.

To my knowledge, those countries we now call 'Eastern' probably have the largest proportion of the world's population, their history goes back for thousands of years, they possess in total many natural treasures and they carry on with life uninhibited by outside influences. They also have the largest collection of old roses in the world.

There is a group of noisette roses in the East German Sangerhausen Rosarium which is simply beautiful. The roses represent every shape, colour and form which was ever created. They repose in beds on the gentle hillside of this historically important garden. They are cared for lovingly by those who work there, and they are catalogued and preserved for all to see. Quite a number of the roses described in the group that follows grow very happily in Sangerhausen. This state-operated rose garden has tens of thousands of people from all over the world visiting each year. They must go away impressed with the friendliness and dedication of the staff, the

amazing collection of roses in all families, and, I trust, take back to their own countries a feeling of gratitude and hope for the future. ■

Anne Marie Côte (1875). A lovely old variety to start with, which was raised by Guillot. Tall-growing and robust, it has large, double flowers of white and pale pink, with carmine-pink on the reverse.
Blanche Duranthon. White is the predominant colour of this old favourite. The large blooms are double and are produced in clusters on a tall-growing plant. Raised by Nabonnand.
▼ **Comtesse de Galard-Béarn** (1894). Bernaix produced this excellent rose. The blooms are large and double and appear on

a vigorous, upright-growing plant. They are bright yellow and have a pink centre.
Daniel Lacombe (1886). This lovely old member of the family was raised by Allard. Its flowers have yellow, pale pink and white and are medium sized and double. Tall growing.
Earl of Eldon (1872). Strongly scented, the large, double blooms are pretty shades of copper-bronze and orange-apricot. Sometimes there is a great variation of colour.
Gruss an Freidberg (1902). Introduced by Rogmanns, this little-known member of the group has deep yellow blooms which are large and double. They have a nice scent. The plant is strong-growing to about 2 metres.

▲ **Lady Clonbrook**. Reputed to
have been raised in Ireland, but
of unknown parentage. Tall-
growing, it has blush-pink,
double blooms.
Lady Emily Peel (1862). From
famous parents, Mme Blanche
Lafitte by Sappho, this
Lacharme-raised hybrid had a
fair measure of popularity in its
day. It is white with light red
shadings and tall growing.
Mme Fanny de Forest (1882).
Introduced by Schwartz, this
lovely hybrid has very large
flowers with plenty of petals.
They are lemon and white and
appear on a medium- to tall-
growing plant.

◀ **Mme Foureau** (1913).
Viaud-Bruant was the raiser of
this more recent hybrid. The
medium-sized, yellow-shaded
flowers are produced freely on
a healthy plant to about 1.5
metres.
Mme François Pittet (1877).
Lightly scented, this pure white
variety was raised by
Lacharme. Tall growing, the
flowers are double and of
medium size.
Mme Gaston Annouilh (1899).
Another fine white hybrid, this
time raised by Chauvry. It has
a strong fragrance and the
blooms are double and medium
sized. It is tall growing.

▲ **Mme Martignier** (1903). Strongly fragrant, this Dubreuil hybrid has three colours prominent: lemon, orange and deep pink. The large double blooms have a nice mix of all three.

Mme Pierre Cochet (1891). Deep yellow, double blooms abound on this tall-growing plant. They are of medium size and nicely fragrant. It was raised by Pierre Cochet.

▲ **Meteor** (1887). This rose, raised by Geschwind, is one of the not-so-common red hybrids. Strongly scented, the large, double flowers are freely produced. Tall growing.

Milkmaid (1925). An Australian hybrid raised by Alister Clark, this rose has some 'Crépuscule' in it. The growth is very vigorous and the blooms are smallish, semi-double, white with some deeper shades. Fragrant.

▲ **Pavillon de Pregny** (1863). In a family packed with beautiful roses it is not surprising to find another one, although this is different. It is purplish-pink and nicely scented. Raised by Guillot.

Souvenir de Lucie (1893). Pinkish-red is the colour of this fine hybrid, raised by Schwartz. It is white, has medium-sized double blooms and grows vigorously.

Triomphe des Noisettes (1887). To finish this group is this excellent rose raised by Pernet. I have grown this variety for several seasons now and have come to much appreciate its purplish-pink, large, double and very fragrant flowers. It is indeed a triumph in every way.

Orange Schoon

Teas and Hybrid Teas

It seems that things do not change much from one century to another. Over 100 years ago Henry Bennett of Manor Farm, Stapleford, Wiltshire, England, finding that farming was not making ends meet, looked for some diversification to augment his income. At the time roses were becoming very popular and if he were to branch out into producing them, it seemed sensible to use some of the facilities he already possessed on the farm as well as acquiring those he would need to make a success of the new venture.

If nothing else, Henry Bennett was a diligent and thoughtful man. It was his habit and his nature to think things out carefully. So he not only purchased roses of the day to observe and grow, but also travelled widely to learn everything he could from the French growers who traditionally raised thousands of roses from self-pollinated seed. The result of this research was that he was quite determined to end the uncertainties of the self-pollination process and do something more scientific which would give him better control over any results he might achieve. He was well received by the French rosarians, who appreciated his sincerity.

Bennett had a number of complications at first, but eventually settled on certain techniques which were to revolutionise the rose-breeding process. Because of the generally inconsistent English climate, outside methods of pollination were fraught with difficulty so he moved the whole system under glass, with all the resultant advantages. He worked among hybrid perpetual and tea roses, and is credited as being the father of the hybrid teas.

Probably the most important rose Bennett raised was the pink hybrid tea 'Lady Mary Fitzwilliam', not because of its show-worthiness but because of its ability to produce excellent seedlings, both directly and indirectly. Thousands of hybrid tea roses owe their existence to this very rose. As with most trail-blazers, it was a long time before this Englishman's work was recognised. It is true that we pass this way but once, and those who love roses should always be grateful that Henry Bennett, erstwhile farmer and successful grower and raiser of roses, did just that. ■

▲ **Amitié** (1951). A very free bloomer which has vigorous, branching, healthy growth. The flowers are large, double and nicely shaped, and are coppery-orange and yellow. A Mallerin hybrid.

▲ **Ariel** (1921). Fragrant, golden-yellow, with occasional streaks of scarlet, describes this rose raised by Bees Ltd of England. The blooms are large, double, and have long stems sitting up very well on a plant with deep green foliage.

Belle Lyonnaise (1870). Reputed to be a seedling from 'Gloire de Dijon', this rose has large, quite double, bright yellow flowers which pale to white. Raised by Levet and is fragrant.

▼ **Chanoine Thaillon** (1931). An old variety which is a strong grower. It has purplish-red buds opening to carmine-red. The flowers are large and double and they have a light scent.

A Celebration of Old Roses

▲ **Comtesse Anne de Bruce**
(1937). Mallerin introduced this
excellent member of the group.
It has different shades of
coppery-orange, pink and red.
The blooms are large, double
and nicely scented.
◀ **Crusader** (1920). This hybrid
has deep green foliage and is a
healthy grower with large, very
double, crimson-scarlet flowers
which are lightly scented.
▶ **Felix Brix** (1921). Quite pretty
shades of salmon-pink, light
yellow and pale pink make up
this rose's large, double flowers
which freely appear on a
medium-sized plant.

▼ **Fernand Arles** (1949). Jean Gaujard raised this rose, which has very large, double, apricot-salmon blooms with a flush of red. They are fragrant and freely produced.

▲ **Frau Eva Schubert** (1937). A pretty little rose which has small, semi-double, pink flowers. They are abundantly produced on a vigorous plant.
Friendship (1938). This fine hybrid was raised by Dickson of Northern Ireland and is not to be confused with another later rose of the same name. Bright red with deeper shades, the flowers are large, double and fragrant.
► **Gloaming** (1935). Here is a rose with famous parents in 'Charles P. Kilham' and 'Mme Pierre S. Du Pont'. The bright-pink, flushed-salmon, very large flowers are also very fragrant.

A Celebration of Old Roses

◄ **Gloria di Roma** (1937). An Italian hybrid which, because of its name, became very popular. Very strong growth supports large, bright scarlet, fragrant flowers.

Isabella Sprunt (1867). Nice to see an old tea rose in this group. Reputed to be a sport from 'Safrano', it has large, double, sulphur-yellow flowers.

► **Korovo** (1931). Coppery peachy-pink is the colour of this old favourite. There was a time when I helped to grow hundreds of this rose. Fragrant and double.

▼ **Lady Margaret Boscawen** (1911). Dickson introduced this fine, very fragrant hybrid. It has pink, large, double flowers in profusion.

▲ **Lafter** (1948). With at least two famous parents, this Brownell introduction is an excellent rose in its own right. Large, double, orange-yellow blooms.

Laurette (1853). Another old tea rose, this time raised by Robert. It is light yellow, large and double.

A Celebration of Old Roses

▲ **Mme Antoine Mari** (1901). Nicely scented, light pink, large flowers which are very double. The attractive flowers are abundantly produced on a plant growing to over 1 metre. **Mme Caristie Martel** (1913). This is from Pernet-Ducher, again produced during the early century's search for yellow garden roses. Very large, double, light yellow.

▲ **Louise Catherine Breslau** (1913). One of the roses produced by Pernet-Ducher in his search for a deep yellow rose. It has some 'Soleil d'Or' in it and the double, fragrant, pink and bronze-orange blooms have a yellow reverse.

▲ **Mme Georges Landard** (1925). Light pink, scented flowers which are double, large and appear freely on a healthy plant.

▲ **Mme G. Forest Colcombet** (1928). Mallerin produced this fine rose, which is not seen very often these days. The blooms are deep crimson-red, large and double.

▲ **Lumière** (1944). Like most rose establishments, the house of Mallerin has produced some excellent roses over the years. This one has large, golden-yellow flowers, shaded red.

▲ **Mme Joseph Bonnaire** (1892). An old hybrid which comes from two excellent old roses in 'Adam' and 'Paul Neyron'. Tall growing, it has very double, very large, bright pink sumptuous flowers.

▲ **Mme Pierre S. Du Pont** (1928). The parents given for this excellent rose probably explain why it was so popular for such a long time: they include 'Ophelia', 'Rayon d'Or' and 'Souvenir de Claudius Pernet'. Its deep golden-yellow, double, fragrant flowers are very freely produced.

▲ **Mme Segond Weber** (1908). When I became interested in roses during World War Two, this was one of the popular pinks grown at that time. It is silvery-pink and strongly scented.

Maryse Kriloff (1958). Raised by Kriloff, this hybrid is also known as 'Lucy Cramphorn'. This rose has crimson-red, large, double blooms with a good fragrance.

▲ **Molly Sharman-Crawford** (1909). A lovely old tea rose. It is strongly scented and has light lemon, double flowers which pale to white. Raised by Dickson.

▲ **Mrs Tresham Gilbey** (1923). This rose has light salmon-pink, well-shaped blooms.

The plant is of medium height and has deep green glossy foliage.

◄ **Octavius Weld**. An old tea of obscure origins. Typical tea-like growth and foliage, with large, fragrant, pale lemon-shaded-pink flowers.

► **Orange Schoon** (1938). More recent than most of the members of this group, but worth a place here. The scented flowers are bright orange, large and semi-double.

▼ **Président Vignet** (1911). Pernet-Duchet, like all dedicated rose hybridists, produced many roses in the pursuit of his objectives. This fine carmine-crimson, large, double variety has a good scent and grows to a medium height.

▲ **Prince Yugala** (1923). Velvety, deep maroon-red flowers from long pointed buds of even deeper colour. The blooms have a light scent and are abundant on a healthy plant.
► **Souvenir de Claudius Pernet** (1919). Raised by Pernet-

Ducher and named after his son, who lost his life in World War One. This fragrant, deep yellow rose has eluded me for more than thirty years and even after a pilgrimage to Le Parc de Bagatelle all I could find was the label.

A Celebration of Old Roses

▲ **Super Congo** (1950). Produced by Meilland, this comparatively modern hybrid has medium-sized flowers, a light scent, and is deep, velvety crimson-scarlet. Good for cutting.

▲ **William R. Smith** (1908).
Apparently this old tea rose is
known under a variety of
names, but that does not lessen
its beauty or its popularity of
yesteryear. Quite fragrant, it
has a yellow base, creamy on
the inside and pink on the
outer.

▶ **Zulu Queen** (1939). A hybrid
from Kordes, coming from two
famous parents, 'Catherine
Kordes' and 'E. G. Hill', this
rose is nicely fragrant. It has
double, deep wine-red blooms
which sit upright on a strong-
growing plant.

Duchesse de Morny

Hybrid Perpetuals and their Hybrids

It has been written that at one time there were more than 3000 varieties in this class. After collecting and examining many hybrid perpetuals over a long period, I have come to realise that I must have seen hundreds of them and that their parentage must be as complex and varied as it could possibly be. If you should doubt the number of roses in this family, I suggest you gain access to two excellent books which came into my possession somewhat fortuitously. I did not know of their existence until unexpectedly they were sent to me by a West German rosarian. The two books are *Rosenlexikon* by August Jäger, and *Die Rose* by Th. Nietner: both contain a wealth of information. The former, believe it or not, lists some 18,000 roses, and a large number of them are remontant hybrids, or, as we know them, hybrid perpetuals. All of the roses in this volume are described to the last detail by a very clever system of letters and symbols. It is not difficult to read the descriptions once you have the letters translated from German into English and you learn to understand what the symbols mean. While avidly working one's way through this tremendously important volume, one begins to realise just how many old roses there really were. I believe the original work was published in 1936 and my copy is a reprint put out by Gustav Weiland of Lubeck in 1983.

Die Rose is a fine book in its own right. It lists around 5000 roses in some detail and many of these are hybrid perpetuals. Apparently, Nietner was a head gardener in Potsdam prior to the publishing of his volume in 1880. He must have been a conscientious gardener and tradesman because his book has been prepared in a most meticulous fashion, very carefully planned and lovingly put together. My copy is the 1983 Verlag Frick edition. We are indeed fortunate to be able to have the use of these fine works so many years after they were first published, for they give us an accurate insight to the thousands of roses of the time. ■

▼ **Abbé Bramérel** (1872). To start this family we have a deep red, medium-to-large double rose with a light scent. It has healthy foliage, good growth and reaches medium height.

► **A. Geoffroy de St Hilaire** (1878). Strongly fragrant, the medium-red flower of this hybrid is about 8 or 9 cm across and double. The plant is tall growing and quite outstanding when in full flower.
Alexandre Dumas (1862). A deep crimson-scarlet variety which was named after the French author. The blooms are medium sized and double, nicely scented and freely produced on a plant which grows to about 1.5 metres.

▲ **Ami Martin** (1906). Of an unusual colour in that it has burned-orange-red blooms which are very large, very double and very fragrant, this rose is vigorous and healthy.
André le Roy d'Angers (1866). Tall and vigorous, this variety has deep violet, large, double blooms produced abundantly on a healthy plant.

▲ **Archill Gonod** (1864). A fine variety, this old hybrid has a strong fragrance. The crimson, double blooms of medium size are abundant on a sturdy plant.

A Celebration of Old Roses

▲ **Baron G. de St Paul** (1894). This is a tall-growing variety which I have seen pegged down and flowering beautifully. Light pink blooms, double and of medium size.

▼ **Baron Haussmann** (1867). Coloured cerise-pink into deeper shades, these flowers are double and of medium size. Not much is known about this hybrid.

▲ **Baron Taylor** (1880). A very pretty deep pink or light red rose. The flowers are large and nicely double. A vigorous, healthy plant supports a good crop of blooms.

▼ **Berthe Baron** (1869). Pink-flushed-white, the large flowers are quite double and nicely formed. They sit well on a healthy plant which grows to medium size.

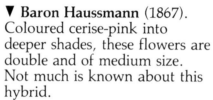

▲ **Bischof Dr Korum** (1922). An unusual member of this family in that it has some yellow in it. The large flowers are double, very fragrant and coloured lemon with light pink.

A Celebration of Old Roses

Black Prince (1866). One of William Paul's introductions. Deep crimson with darker shades is the colour of the large, cupped, double flowers, which are strongly fragrant. Vigorous growth.

▲ **Comte de Mortemart** (1880). Another fine pink rose. The blooms are large and quite double, have a strong fragrance and appear abundantly on a tall-growing plant.

▼ **Comtesse O'Gorman** (1888). Most of the French hybridists of the day had a hand in the additions to this family. This one was raised by Leveque. The plant is of medium height and the reddish-violet flowers are double and large.

Cornet (1848). This variety from Lacharme is pink and has deeper shadings. The flowers, very large and double, are quite fragrant. An excellent old rose.

► **Countess of Oxford** (1869). Deep red, double, large, rounded flowers appear freely on a healthy plant. Raised by Guillot, this hybrid is nicely scented.

▼ **Crown Prince** (1880). Another hybrid raised by William Paul. Coloured deep purple and carmine, the very double blooms have a nice fragrance.

▲ **Dembrowski** (1849). Here we have a fine hybrid, raised by Vibert. Of medium size and reddish-carmine in the flower, the rose is tall growing and healthy.

◄ **Denise Hélye** (1864). This rose was introduced by Gautreau, a new name on our raisers' list. A strong-growing plant supports a fine crop of large, double, pinkish-red blooms.

► **Directeur Alphand** (1885). Also known as 'Alsace Lorraine' this once very popular variety was raised by Leveque. It is tall growing and healthy and has deep purple-red, large, double blooms.

A Celebration of Old Roses

▲ **Dr Andry** (1864). Raised by Verdier, this lovely hybrid comes from 'Charles Lefébvre' and 'Victor Verdier'. Reddish-pink is the colour of the medium-sized, double blooms.

▲ **Duchesse de Cambaceres**
(1854). This rose was raised by
Fontaine and has medium-

sized, double blooms, mostly
lilac-pink, with centres of
purplish-red. It has a nice scent.

▲ **Duchesse de Morny** (1863).
There is no doubt that the
French hybridists were prolific
raisers of hybrid perpetuals.
This one comes from Verdier.
A vigorous grower, it has
large, medium-pink, double
flowers.

◄ **Duhamel Dumonceau**
(1872). Hugues was the raiser
of this hybrid. Quite vigorous
growth supports medium-red,
large, double blooms which
have a good scent.

▼ **Emily Laxton** (1878). A
Laxton-raised rose, this is a
seedling from 'Jules Margottin'.
It has bright red and pink
double blooms. Remontant, it
grows to over 1 metre high.

A Celebration of Old Roses

▲ **Granny Grimmetts** (1955). A much more recent introduction which was put out by Hilling. It has a nice scent and on a tall plant bears medium flowers which are double and deep purple-red in colour.

► **Hans Mackart** (1885). From the house of Verdier. This hybrid is crimson-scarlet, large in the flower and double. The upright, healthy plant supports well-scented blooms.

Hold Slunci (1956). It was generally agreed that there were no yellow varieties in this family, until Blatna raised this rose. Light yellow, double, fragrant blooms grace a compact plant.

▼ **Jules Barigny** (1886). If the story about the French growers lining out tens of thousands of seedlings in the fields is true, then this may explain why there are so many in this group. Verdier raised this strongly scented, crimson, double hybrid.

▲ **Lady Stuart** (1851). White and light pink is the colour of this old hybrid, raised by Portemer. It has large, double blooms which are nicely fragrant.

◄ **Lamotte Sanguin** (1869). Vigneron introduced this fine old variety. Very large, double flowers of deepish carmine-red appear in dark green foliage on a tall-growing plant.

▼ **Léon Delaville** (1885). Verdier must have been a very busy man. In many of the families, he has been credited with hundreds of hybrids. This one is deep crimson with double flowers.

Magna Charta (1876). William
Paul was responsible for the
introduction of some very good
roses and this is one of them. It
has pinkish-red, very large
flowers with a nice scent.
► **Mme Louis Ricard** (1904).
Large, double, bright pink
blooms are freely produced on
a vigorous plant. Raised by
Boutigny, this hybrid is of
more recent origins.
▼ **Mlle Honorine Duboc**
(1894). Of medium height, this
variety has double, very large
flowers of rich, deep pink.
Raised by Duboc.

▼ **Mlle Marie Magat** (1889).
Liabaud is credited with this
fine variety. Light red blooms,
which are large and double,
cover a vigorous, tall-growing
plant.

▼ **Mlle Thérèse Levet** (1864).
Bright pink blooms with a
medium scent are freely
produced. They are large and
very double. A Levet hybrid.

▲ **Monsieur de Morand** (1891). A hybrid from Schwartz, this has medium pink, large and double blooms covering a healthy, tall-growing plant.
Monsieur Ernest Dupré (1904). The second rose raised by Boutigny in this group. Another good red, with large, double blooms abundantly produced on a medium-sized plant.

▶ **Monsieur Hoste** (1884). Not just another red rose, but a particularly fine variety from 'Baron de Bonstetten'. Raised by Liabaud, and the second from this source.
▼ **Mrs F. W. Sandford** (1898). Strongly scented, this rose is tall growing. It has large, very double blooms of light pink, produced over a long period.

Panachée de Bordeaux (1898). We have known 'Ferdinand Pichard' as an excellent striped member of this family. This hybrid from Duprat has red and white striped flowers which are large and double.

◄ **Panachée d'Orléans** (1854). It seems fitting that we should follow with another striped rose, this time from Wilhelm. The medium-scented, large flowers are light pink with deep pink stripes.

▼ **Prince Henri d'Orléans** (1886). Another Verdier origination, this useful and distinctive rose of medium height has pale red, large blooms with a light scent.

Princesse Marie Dolgorouky (1878). The third of the striped roses in this group. Raised by Gonod, this is a vigorous rose growing to at least 1.5 metres. It bears very large blooms of light pink with red stripes.

◄ **Star of Waltham** (1875). William Paul raised this rose, which became one of the most popular of the class. The nicely scented, very large flowers are crimson-red and double.

► **Triomphe d'Alençon** (1858). Medium-pink, large flowers, double and scented, appear freely on a medium-growing, healthy plant. Touvais is the raiser.

Victor Hugo (1884). This is a well known rose which it is nice to see again. Raised by Schwartz, the blooms are deep crimson with purple shades at times and have a good scent.

▼ **Violette Bouyer** (1881). Lacharme was the introducer of this last rose in this group. It comes from two fine parents in 'Jules Margottin' and 'Sombreuil'. It has large, double, scented, white-shaded-pink flowers.

Rosa Zwerg

Rugosas and their Hybrids

There is no doubt that this family of roses is becoming more and more popular. Added to this, of course, is the fact that recently quite a few hybridists have turned their attention in this direction. What has become known as the 'Explorer' series has been created by Dr Felicitas Svejda, who emigrated from Vienna to Canada in 1953. She soon realised that much of Canada had a very harsh climate not at all suited to rose culture. Most modern roses found the environment intolerable and, even when soil was heaped up around the plants to protect them from winter kill, they were lucky to survive.

In 1961 Dr Svejda began a breeding programme to develop roses with the extreme hardiness of the rugosas and the prolific flowering ability of the modern garden rose. She worked under the auspices of the Plant Research Centre of the Central Experimental Farm in Ottawa and chose to call the new hybrids after the early explorers in Canadian history. In 1969, using 'Schneezwerg', a rugosa hybrid, 'Martin Frobisher', the first of the series, was produced, and both of these roses are dealt with in my first book.

The year 1968 saw a switch to a different breeding direction. 'R. kordesii' was used with a local seedling, and 'John Cabot' was the result. Then followed the rest of the 'Explorer' group. Although these roses are technically quite new, they are old in their concept; all are dealt with in some detail in the group which now follows. Dr Svejda has now retired and Dr Ian Ogilvie will carry on the 'Explorer' series research in L'Assomption, Quebec. The new group as a whole has become very popular and it seems that Canadian nurseries have not been able to keep up with the demand for plants. European growers are producing them in quantity, and it seems rather fitting that plants of the 'Explorer' series are now being sent back to Canada from Europe in the same way in which the early explorers left Europe to discover Canada.

It must be noted at this point that the 'Explorer' series may or may not have rugosa blood in their veins, because information on them is very disjointed. However, for the sake of convenience they are all included in this family. ■

Alexander Mackenzie. One of the 'Explorer' series raised by Dr Felicitas Svejda. This hybrid is one of the most hardy and disease-resistant of the group. It will easily reach 2 metres in height and has double, crimson-scarlet, medium-sized blooms in profusion.

Alice Aldrich (1899). A hybrid raised by Lovett. It is not tall growing but has a nice scent. Double, cerise-pink flowers of medium size are freely produced.

America (1894). Typical of the rugosa family, with the beautiful foliage and the attractive oval fruit. The large flowers are almost single and coloured a pretty carmine-pink. Raised by W. Paul.

▼ Champlain (1982). This rose may well have little or no rugosa in it, but is grouped here with the others of the Canadian 'Explorer' series. Brilliant, deep scarlet, double flowers appear prolifically in large clusters on a compact plant.

A Celebration of Old Roses

Charles Albanel. Again, a Svejda hybrid, this time of low-growing habit, excellent for ground cover, and bearing double, red flowers in great numbers over a long season.
Cibles (1894). A very old hybrid, raised by Dr Kaufmann, and the parentage is given as *R. rugosa rubra* by 'Perle de Lyon'. The light carmine flowers have a yellow centre and are medium sized, fragrant and single.
David Thompson. Another hybrid from the 'Explorer' series raised by Dr Svejda. This group of roses has been proven hardy for the coldest climates. Fragrant, light red, double flowers on a healthy plant.
Georges Cain (1909). 'Pierre Notting' and *R. rugosa* are given as the parents of this Jules Gravereaux hybrid. It has deep blood-red, double flowers with lilac-pink shades and is quite beautiful.
Germanica (1900). Raised by Dr Muller, this rose's flowers are deep violet-red, quite double and nicely fragrant. The plant is not tall growing but is healthy and disease-resistant.
▼ **Henry Hudson.** From the 'Explorer' series. A fine hybrid of comparatively short growth. It has double, white, medium-sized flowers which are flushed pink.

Henry Kelsey. 'Explorer' series. This variety can be classed as a climber. It grows to about 3 metres and has an abundance of double, bright-red blooms.

▼ **Jens Munk.** This is another rose from the 'Explorer' series. Medium-pink blooms on a plant growing at least 2 metres high.

▲ **John Cabot**. 'Explorer' series. Arching branches on a tall growing plant carry many semi-double, red flowers. A Silver Medal award-winning climber which has become very well known. John Cabot was a Genoese navigator and explorer.

John Davis. 'Explorer' series. Disease resistance and an abundance of blooms are the hallmarks of this hybrid. It has double-pink blossoms which are quite fragrant.

John Franklin A compact, healthy grower to about 1 metre. It has large clusters of up to thirty blooms which are double, red and fragrant. John Franklin lost his life in an attempt to discover the North West Passage to Canada.

Mme Ancelot (1910). Of mixed parentage, this lovely old variety is very fragrant and the medium-sized flowers are double and white with pink shades. Tall growing.

▶ **Mme Ph. Plantamour** (1900). This, too, is an old and useful hybrid. It is tall growing and has semi-double, medium to large flowers which are of deep red colour.

Mercedes (1900). Guillot was the raiser of this unusual rugosa rose, with pink, red and white colour prominently displayed. It is scented, with medium-sized, double flowers.

Montblanc. The first of a group from Baum of West Germany. Pure white, double flowers, pink in the middle and with a very strong scent. It has the usual large, orange-red fruit and grows to about 1 metre.

▲ **Monte Cassino**. Semi-double, cerise-pink to cerise-red, medium-sized flowers appear profusely on a plant about 1 metre high. They are strongly fragrant, and a nice crop of fruit follows. A Baum hybrid.

Monte Rosa. This hybrid has large, carmine-pink flowers which are lightly double. As always with this family, they appear over a long season. Orange-red fruit in profusion. Another Baum hybrid.

▲ **Nyveldt's White** (1955). Over the years *Rugosa alba* has held pride of place as a very popular single white. This rose is another of the same type, except that the stamens are a lighter yellow and the foliage is a paler green.

► **Rosa Zwerg**. Quite short for a member of this family. Grows to about 45 cm and strongly scented. The blooms are a nice pink, lightly double and small-to-medium in size. A Baum variety.

◄ **Rötes Meer**. Again, a short grower, and an introduction by Baum. Carmine-pink, double, strongly scented blooms appear abundantly, followed by orange-red fruit.

▲ **Schneekoppe.** The sixth of the Baum hybrids, short and compact in growth. All are excellent for low hedge and edges. Strongly scented, double, white blooms emerge from pale pink buds.

▲ **Semi-double Scarlet**. Seizo Suzuki, of Japan, over a period of years has raised many roses of many kinds and here in succession are three rugosa hybrids which are very attractive in several ways.

'Semi-double Scarlet' has bright scarlet flowers, about 8 cm across, notable for a nice group of light-yellow stamens and a good scent.

▶ **Single Pink**. Bearing a flower comprising just five petals, this Seizo Suzuki hybrid is pale carmine pink, with light green foliage.

▲ **Single White**. The third hybrid from Seizo Suzuki, this one has pure white, single flowers about the same size as the two preceding roses. It is nicely fragrant. All three have light green foliage and are healthy growers.

Souvenir de Yeddo (1874). A lovely old variety, not seen very often these days. Grows to about 1 metre and is given as a hybrid from *R. rugosa* and *R. odorata*. It has double blooms of an attractive pink, shaded white.

Stella Polaris (1890). Jensen is the raiser of this lovely hybrid which is a good grower, with fern-like foliage and arching branches. These are adorned by double, white, cupped blooms in clusters of three to five.

Stern von Prag (1924). The parentage of this rose is given as an *R. rugosa* seedling and 'Edward Mawley'. As the latter rose is very dark crimson, it is only to be expected that this hybrid should be deep red too. The flowers are double, fragrant and freely produced.

Tetonkaha (1912). A fine hybrid raised by Professor Hansen, this is deep pink, semi-double, very fragrant, and has a long flowering season.

▲ **William Baffin** (1983). 'Explorer' series. This rose is almost continuous flowering. It is very hardy and disease-resistant. The semi-double blooms, crimson above and silvery below, are medium sized and produced in clusters.

William Baffin was a navigator and explorer, born in London in 1584. In 1612 he was chief pilot of an expedition attempting to discover the North West Passage. Later, under Captain Bylot's command on the *Discovery*, Baffin Bay was named after him.

Sally Holmes

Hybrid Musks and Varieties

Generally, the credit for the creation of this class goes to the Englishman Joseph Pemberton, and Peter Lambert, of Germany, but there were others, of course, including Wilhelm Kordes, George C. Thomas, Francis E. Lester and J. A. Bentall. It is accepted that most, if not all, of the hybrid musks which carry the name of Bentall were raised by Pemberton. After the latter's death, the unreleased hybrids were put out by Bentall.

The American George C. Thomas also worked with roses of this family in California. He was responsible for raising up to fifty hybrids and, for about ten or twelve of them, hybrid musks were used as one parent, mostly 'Danae' and 'Moonlight'. Again we are faced with the problem of trying to classify these roses correctly. Most of them could be placed in this class, but perhaps they could just as easily be with the noisettes or hybrid teas. 'Bloomfield Dainty' was dealt with in the second book of this series and is probably better known, but there are some lovely roses from G. C. Thomas in the group that follows.

When talking and writing about Peter Lambert and his association with the founding of the rosarium at Sangerhausen it must be mentioned that there were other men involved. Probably the most prominent of these was Albert Hoffman. He was one of the prime movers in the venture, and if you are fortunate enough to visit the state rosarium you will find a very fine bronze plaque as a memorial to him, nestled quietly in the rear of one of the beds. One wonders, while standing there, what thoughts the old gentleman would have if it were possible for him to see the gardens today.

Doubtless he would be proud to know that the work he helped to start is going on in the best possible way almost 100 years later. It is carried out by a devoted and caring staff led by the Director of Rosariums, Ingomar Lang. ■

Bloomfield Comet (1924). A fine single rose, with flowers about 9 cm across, comes from 'Duchess of Wellington' and 'Danae'. The buds are long pointed, orange-red, and the five-petalled flowers are fragrant and open a nice shade of orange with yellow in the centre.

Bloomfield Culmination (1924). This also comes from 'Danae', and the single, 8 cm blooms are lightly scented. It flowers over a long season from pointed buds opening to a pleasant rose-pink shade, paling to white in the middle.

Bloomfield Dawn (1931). Tall growing, this hybrid has quite large semi-double blooms with a bicolour effect. They are nicely fragrant, light pink on the inside and deep pink on the outer.

Bloomfield Discovery (1925). Again a 'Danae' seedling with large, 8 cm single flowers, bright pink on the inner petals and a deeper pink on the outer. The plant is a medium grower and has deep green, shiny foliage.

Bloomfield Fascination (1924). A profuse bloomer, this lovely variety comes from parents 'Danae' and the china 'Madame Laurette Messimy'. The small, double flowers appear freely and are light yellow. The plant grows well, with light green foliage.

Bloomfield Favourite (1924). Here is a hybrid from 'Moonlight' and the rambler 'Debutante'. The blooms are nicely double, of a pleasant pink and cream, with a light scent.

Bloomfield Perfection (1925). 'Danae' again is one of the parents of this fine variety. The double flowers are quite different in that they are creamy yellow with a shading of lilac-pink. They have a light scent.

▲ **Cascadia** (1925). For a rose to receive the Portland Gold Medal it must be of a certain quality. This is a vigorous, free-flowering grower and has small, semi-double blooms which are blush-pink fading to white.
All of the foregoing roses were raised by George C. Thomas of California.

Eponine. This is quite double, with lovely cupped, pure white flowers which are strongly fragrant.

Galatea (1914). One of Pemberton's early hybrids which we do not hear much about these days. Probably the result of his first efforts at hybridising. It has a long flowering season, small rosette flowers in clusters, and has greyish-amber and pink shades.

Havering (1937). This hybrid is credited to Bentall and was named after the home of Joseph Pemberton, who employed him. The flowers appear in clusters of four or five. They are large, china-pink in colour and very fragrant.

Herrenhausen (1938). A fine hybrid from Kordes. With parents like 'Eva' and 'Golden Rapture', it could hardly be anything else. The large, double flowers are light yellow, fading lighter, and come from greenish-yellow buds. Nicely fragrant.

▲ **Lessing** (1914). Bred from 'Trier', which was the rose that Joseph Pemberton used as a base for his hybridising. Large clusters of small, double, nicely fragrant flowers of deep rose-pink with white markings and a lemon centre.

▲ **Marjorie Fair** (1978). 'Ballerina' and 'Baby Faurax' are the parents of this fairly recent hybrid from the house of Harkness. You may be surprised to see this rose in this family, but it has just as much right as many others. The

small, deep red, single flowers in clusters are freely produced. **Miriam** (1919). Could be classified as a hybrid tea but is quite at home here in this family. The flowers are freely produced, double, lightly scented, and orange-yellow.

▲ **Madeleine Lemoine**. Quite old, this hybrid is a bit of a mystery. It is reputed to come from *R. moschata* and *R. gigantea*. The flowers are large, a little more than single, creamy-white and very fragrant.

▲ **Pearl** (1915). Pale pink, lemon and white small flowers in large clusters. The light-coloured flowers in the different shades

make a very pretty combination. The plant is vigorous, tall growing and healthy.

Princesse de Nassau (1835). A very early variety from Laffay. The blooms are very double, medium sized, with lemon-yellow and white shades. They are fragrant and the plant is vigorous.

Rosaleen (1932). Another hybrid attributed to Bentall. It has double, crimson-red blooms which appear profusely in large clusters. The plant is healthy, growing vigorously to about 2 metres.

▲ **Sally Holmes** (1976). The parents of this fine hybrid are 'Ivory Fashion' and 'Ballerina'. One of the prettiest roses to have come on the scene for a long time, it has lightly scented, quite large flowers, 9 cm across, single and creamy-white in colour. Plentiful bloom.

▼ **Sammy** (1921). Blooms repeatedly and has a light scent. The small, little more than single flowers are cerise-pink and are produced in

profusion on a tall plant. A Pemberton hybrid.

Sea Spray (1923). Joseph Pemberton was responsible for this variety, too. The small, double, white blooms sometimes have a flush of pink in them and appear in clusters on a vigorous plant.

▼ **Sissi Ketten** (1900). Raised by Ketten, this hybrid comes from 'Mignonette' and the tea rose 'Safrano'. The flowers at the base are lemon and white, with pink and carmine shades overlaid. They are medium sized and quite pretty in their own way. Seems to fit better in this family than anywhere else.

Snowstorm (1908). As expected, this hybrid has pure white flowers, semi-double and small. They are set up on a strong, healthy plant in large clusters. Raised by W. Paul.

Maiwunder

Shrub-climbers and their Relatives

This family has in the past been a matter for concern and debate. The roses in this group have always been of very mixed ancestry and often it is difficult to say whether they belong here or in some other classification. Nevertheless, those that are included here this time are just as varied as before. Also appearing in this list are some that are referred to as groundcover or procumbent types. It is true that these roses will cover quite an area of ground, but it is also true that, given a little bit of assistance, they can be made to climb most successfully, hence their inclusion here.

Appearing in this family are a number of roses raised by Dr Griffith Buck who, under the jurisdiction of Iowa State University, has been working for many years now in an endeavour to create winter-hardy roses. One of his earlier introductions, 'Applejack', grows untended in our garden at the present and has reached nearly 3 metres across and tall. It never seems to be without flower among its apple-scented foliage. Dr Buck has introduced many varieties, most of which have been released by the firm known as 'Roses of Yesterday and Today', of Watsonville, California. Indeed it is a pleasure to visit their display garden in Brown's Valley Road and see most of Griffith Buck's roses doing very well there. On the short but steep path up to the office you can admire groups of these roses, which you most likely will not find anywhere else.

Also presented in the family which follows are four roses bred by Toru Onodera of Japan, including the beautiful and now very well known 'Nozomi'. Here, too, we have a gentle man who has lost his head and his heart to the genus Rosa. ■

◀ **Akashi** (1968). The first of Toru Onodera's hybrids, this is a sister seedling to 'Nozomi' and has the same look and habit except for the flowers, which are very double, small and a bright cerise-pink. It makes an excellent weeping standard and, like its sister, is quite procumbent.

▼ **Amiga Mia** (1979). A hardy shrub-type rose which was raised by Griffith Buck. Repeat flowering on upright, long stems, the large, double blooms of rich bright pink with a white base are quite fragrant. An excellent variety.

A Celebration of Old Roses

▲ **April Moon** (1982). Long, yellow buds open to large, 12 cm, quite double flowers of white with lemon at the base. The blooms appear in twos and threes on a tall-growing, vigorous plant with deep green leaves. This is a Buck hybrid.

▲ **Christine Wright** (1909). The bright pink, large, fragrant flowers are semi-double and have a nice group of golden stamens. This vigorous plant has glossy green foliage.

Coral Dawn (1952). This fine variety comes from 'New Dawn' and two unknown roses. At 10–12 cm, the double blooms are quite large. On a strong-growing plant the clusters of bright pink, fragrant flowers are produced freely.

Dreamgirl (1944). Another excellent hybrid for this class. The strongly scented, very double blooms are a pretty salmon-pink with shades of apricot. The plant is vigorous and the foliage is shiny.

Earth Song (1976). Soft rose pink with deeper shadings and copper is the colour of another Buck rose. Excellent for picking, the nicely shaped buds come in clusters on a healthy plant.

Enchanted Autumn (1976). One thing Buck's roses are never short of is imaginative names. Deep coral-pink, shaded red, large blooms which are strongly scented. The clusters are from one to three and the foliage is bronze and green.

Étain (1953). Now and again we come across a very hardy rose and this is one of them. It sends out long trailers which are generously supplied with lightly scented, 8 cm, salmon-pink flowers.

► **Frontier Twirl** (1979). Very modern in its concept, this Buck hybrid stands out among all the others of his raising. Deep salmon-pink buds open to medium salmon, double blooms of hybrid-tea shape. Freely produced on a healthy plant.

Hawkeye Belle (1975). Another Buck variety, this is a profuse performer. The quite large, 15 cm flowers are double and very well scented. Coloured white, sometimes blush and pale-lemon tinted, the blooms appear well-set in deep green foliage.

▼ **Honey Sweet**. It has to be a Buck variety with such a name. The big, deep salmon flowers are produced freely on a large plant. It is beautiful in every stage.

Le Rêve (1933). Not unlike 'Lawrence Johnstone', to which it has some relationship, this variety's semi-double, large, pale yellow flowers are fragrant and quite beautiful when at their best on a happy-looking plant.

▲ **Maiwunder**. This is a lovely shrub rose raised by Kordes. It is upright in growth and has light green foliage. The flowers are large, coming from pointed buds which are purplish-pink in colour, with rolled edges to the petals. It is nicely fragrant.

▶ **Marie Bugnet** (1963). This rose is a very hardy variety which has pure white, very fragrant, 8 cm flowers. The growth is compact and bushy and the foliage is rugosa-like. All in all, a most beautiful and useful rose.

Maytime (1975). It has been said that this could be the finest of Griffith Buck's introductions. 'Maytime' has long, pointed buds of deep apricot-pink which open to a lighter shaded, 10 cm, semi-double flower. Lightly fragrant.

► **Miyagino** (1968). Another sister seedling of Onodera's 'Nozomi'. Growth habit, foliage and prickles almost identical to the former. The flowers are different, but only just — single pink, about 3 cm across, and with a lighter-coloured centre.

A Celebration of Old Roses

◄ **Mountain Music**. Another Buck hybrid, this time with large, double, lilac-pink flowers at first; when opening shows some buffy lemon in the throat. Grows into a large, healthy shrub and blooms freely.

▼ **Mountain Snow** (1985). Large clusters of white flowers cascade down a very vigorous plant which grows up to 6 metres. The foliage is the darkest green and the blooms are semi-double with golden stamens.

Music Maker (1972). Not a tall grower, this Buck variety has masses of blooms in clusters. They are nicely formed, fragrant double flowers, soft pink in the bud, becoming quite pale later.

▲ **Night Song** (1978). Probably one of the brightest of the Buck roses, and not unlike a David Austin hybrid. It has large, very double, bright crimson-scarlet flowers which appear singly on long stems. Healthy foliage on a strong plant.

► **Nozomi** (1968). Single blooms of just five petals that are quite rosy pink in the bud, opening to blush-pink and paling to white, about 3 cm across. The foliage is healthy and plentiful and the growth is vigorous, arching and tenacious. Given the chance and the space the plant will spread densely to about 2 metres. The arrival of this rose, which was raised by Toru Onodera from 'Fairy Princess' and 'Sweet Fairy', has had, and will have, a profound effect on the genus Rosa. If followed through, it could be the first of a new class.

Toro Onodera was born in 1913. His father was a high school teacher in Nagoya and his mother was a teacher of the Japanese tea ceremony and Ikebana. Toru's love of flowers seems to have been developed through her influence. Even during World War Two he was known to collect seeds and flowers. In about 1960 he began hybridising roses and his first successful rose was 'Nozomi'. He named this hybrid after his niece who, at the age of four, lost her life in one of the atomic blasts during the war. He has since raised many hybrids and has had many successes, and he must be one of Japan's most successful amateur rose growers. His philosophy includes the belief that roses are the children of the sun and of Nature. He says he has a never-ending dream when it comes to rose breeding and sees truth and beauty in Nature.

▲ **Orange Ruffels** (1952). A vigorous and healthy plant with glossy foliage. The freely produced flowers are large, double, very fragrant and of an attractive orange colour, lighter at the base.

▲ **Paloma Blanca**. Quite rosy-pink buds develop into most beautiful white, double flowers with pale lemon down in the throat. The plant grows quite large, to nearly 2 metres.

Pearlie Mae (1982). Named for entertainer Pearl Bailey by Griffith Buck, the hybrid-tea-like flowers are deep pink in the bud, opening to golden-yellow with a flush of salmon.

Pink Pillar (1940). Three or more quite double flowers in a cluster of pink, coral and orange, with a citrus perfume. The growth of the plant is vigorous and healthy. Makes an excellent shrub.

Prairie Flower (1975). Having a light scent, the almost single flower opens flat to about 8 cm across, cardinal red with a white centre. They appear continually on an upright plant.

▲ **Prairie Harvest**. Griffith Buck has excelled himself with this variety. It is deep yellow in its long, pointed buds, opening to lemon-yellow flowers, paling on the edges and deliciously scented. The stems are long, with blooms usually one per stem. Light green foliage.

Radox Bouquet (1981). This hybrid combines the fragrance of old garden roses with the repeat-flowering habit of the modern. Its warm rose-pink, double flowers are freely produced on a healthy, upright plant.

Red Blanket (1979). Not a big grower, but this rose makes an ever-blooming shrub which produces semi-double, medium-sized red flowers in clusters. An Ilsink hybrid.

▶ **Rosy Cushion** (1979). Again not a big grower, and from the same source, Ilsink of Holland,

this has medium-sized, semi-double flowers which are pink with a white centre.

September Song (1980). A tall-growing shrub with a beautiful flowering display. The bud is deep apricot, opening to paler peach and apricot, with pink at the edges of the petals. The flowers are double and very fragrant. A Buck rose.

Serendipity (1979). Buff-yellow with pink shades and a very strong apple fragrance. The name implies the knack of stumbling upon interesting discoveries, undoubtedly an aptitude of its creator, Griffith Buck.

▼ **Silver Shadows**. I feel this Buck variety will be one of the most popular when it is better known. Tall growing and healthy, the plant sends up pointed buds of greyish-mauve opening to lilac-mauve. These flowers are beautifully fragrant.

▲ **Suma**. This is the third of the sister seedlings of Onodera's 'Nozomi'. Like the other two, it has growth habits and foliage appearance similar to 'Nozomi' but differs in its small, profuse, very double, carmine-pink flowers.

Summer Wind (1975). It was not intended that this family should turn out to be an advertisement for Griffith Buck of Iowa State University. If it should appear that way then it is richly deserved. This Griffith Buck hybrid has deep green foliage and large, semi-double flowers of deep orange-red with yellow at the base.

Utersen (1978). Correctly called 'Rosarium Utersen', this is a fairly recent introduction from Kordes. Nicely fragrant, and disease-resistant, it has blooms in deep tones of bright pink and is very free flowering.

▼ **Weetwood** (1983). Extremely strong growing, up to 7 or more metres, this is a seedling from 'Debutante'. It has large hanging trusses of delicate pink, double blooms which are of rosette formation.

▲ **White Cockade** (1969). An excellent, free-standing plant if you wish, or a slow climber if desired, this comes from Cocker and has attractive hybrid-tea-shaped, large, fragrant white blooms which appear almost continuously.

▶ **Wiesse Gruss an Aachen** (1944). As the parent of this variety was placed in this category in the first book of this series, it seems proper to place the pure white sport of it here too. This rose has a nice scent and in every other way resembles its parent.

Wild Ginger (1976). Its colour is different shadings of orange, apricot, yellow and copper. The quite contemporary colourings sit well among the deep bronzy foliage of a healthy plant. Why not conclude this family with another Buck rose?

Else Poulsen

Polyanthas and their Relatives

Once again we present a useful collection of polyantha roses. It must be remembered that this class began in 1875 and moved on over many years, with perhaps the most productive period being between 1910 and 1920. Like all rose families, these have led on to families of the future. In this case the polyanthas led us into the hybrid polyanthas and on to the floribundas.

There were many raisers involved in the polyantha's development, among them Guillot, Lambert, Levavasseur, Turbat, Pernet-Ducher, Dubreuil, Bernaix, Soupert & Notting, Bennett, Schmidt, Poulsen, Nonin, de Ruiter and Kordes. Remember that all of these growers and hybridists were concerned with other rose families as well. In my second book I made the suggestion that I would like to see this family taken in hand by modern hybridists and some work done in this direction. The possibilities are tremendous.

In an article written by Walter Easlea, for the 1916 edition of the *Rose Annual*, he said, 'The usefulness of the polyanthas is only now being fully realized. I think they will largely displace bedding plants and they certainly are the most economical plant one can utilize, for after the initial outlay there is no further expense for years; and [they] have the double advantage in that slight frosts will not harm them, and they appear brilliant the next day following a downpour. In conclusion I would just say a word or two as to the possibilities of the polyantha roses, and would urge our own hybridists not to devote all their skill to the development of the Hybrid Teas and Teas, but to give some attention to these lovely little polyanthas.'

The development Walter Easlea asked for, and for which I unwittingly repeated a request seventy years later, is at last near at hand. The breeding houses of the world are working along these lines at this very moment, and there are available even now many roses created from the parentage discussed here. I cannot but wonder what lies ahead. Of one thing we can be sure, however — there will be many beautiful roses along the way. ■

► **Baby Betty** (1929). A great little hybrid with which to start this family. Compact, bushy growth and deep, shiny foliage which has an excellent long-flowering season. The small, double, fragrant flowers are pink, shaded lighter at the base, and the buds are yellowish with red edging.
Baby Chatenay (1914). This pretty variety is from a cross between 'Mme A. Chatenay' and 'Mme Norbert Levavasseur' and leans towards the former in its looks. Light pink, double flowers on a compact plant.

Baby Elegance (1912). Single, light yellowish-orange blooms form nice upright clusters on a medium-sized plant with healthy foliage. Unusual.
Baby Farben Koenigin (1913). Another lovely little rose raised from 'Mme Norbert Levavasseur', the other parent being 'Farben Koenigin'. Small, deep pink, double blooms appear profusely on a hardy plant.

▼ **Dairy Maid** (1957). A pretty hybrid from E. B. LeGrice with quite yellow buds in clusters, opening cream and fading to white in large, single blooms which sometimes have carmine-pink markings.

▲ **Dorothy Howarth** (1921). It is hard to believe that this medium-sized, bright pink variety comes from 'Leonie Lamesch'. It must be that the other parent, 'Annchen Müller', has more influence and this is where the colour, fragrance and glossy foliage comes from.

Éblouissant (1918). During a recent visit to Denmark I was struck by the beauty of this little rose, and when you realise that 'Cramoisi Supérieure' is one of its parents, perhaps this explains why. A very showy, ever blooming, dwarf, deep crimson-scarlet with a light scent.

Else Poulsen (1924). One of the many excellent roses introduced by Poulsens, the prolific firm of Danish rose hybridisers. Semi-double, bright rose-pink, medium-sized blooms, readily produced on a long stem.

Étoile d'Or (1899). Citron yellow is the colour of this Dubreuil-raised hybrid. A fairly old rose which is not seen much these days, it is quite hardy. The blooms are medium-sized and double and spread over a long season.

Étoile de Mai (1893). A very pretty little rose which is forever in flower. Its double, very fragrant, lemon and white blooms are borne in many clusters.

Gloire d'Orléans (1912). One of Levavasseur's hybrids. The deep red, double, small flowers are produced freely on a medium-sized healthy plant.

Golden Salmon Supérieure (1929). Many of the polyantha class were created by their ability to sport, both in colour and in form. This very deep orange sport, with small flowers in clusters on a strong plant, is one of them.
Jeanny Soupert (1912). The small, double, white-shaded-light-pink flowers are produced in clusters over a long season. This is from 'Mme Norbert Levavasseur' and 'Petite Leonie'.
Jessie (1909). Bright crimson, lightening to pink, semi-double flowers about 4 cm across which are white in the middle and lightly scented. The plant is compact, with shiny foliage.

▲ **Kirsten Poulsen** (1924). When a rose appears which is different from those already in cultivation, it is not always realised that it could be the commencement of a new family. This Poulsen-produced single scarlet, with others from the same raiser, was one of the first hybrid polyanthas.

A Celebration of Old Roses

Maman Levavasseur (1907). A sport from 'Mme Norbert Levavasseur', this has bright reddish-pink, double flowers in clusters on a medium-growing, healthy plant. Has also been called 'Baby Dorothy'.

Maman Turbat (1911). Again 'Mme Norbert Levavasseur' is used as a parent with the beautiful 'Katharina Zeimet'. Quite a sizeable flower, in large clusters, bright pink and mauve, with white underneath. Compact, healthy plant.

Martha (1906). A low-growing plant supports small double flowers of bronze and pink in large clusters. It has two fine roses for parents in 'Thalia' and 'Mme Laurette Messimy', the first a rambler, the second a china.

▼ **Mme Norbert Levavasseur** (1903). Probably the raiser of this rose, Levavasseur, did not realise what an important rose he had created with this hybrid. From 'Crimson Rambler' and 'Gloire des Polyantha', this hybrid has crimson-scarlet, small, semi-double blooms in a large cluster. They tend to blue and are lightly fragrant. There is no doubt that this rose, more than any other, helped to establish the class firmly. Unfortunately some confusion arose with extra names when it was called 'Red Baby Rambler', while 'Maman Levavasseur' was

called 'Pink Baby Rambler' or 'Baby Dorothy', and 'Katharina Zeimet' became 'White Baby Rambler'. It has been suggested that these names were substituted for promotional purposes. Notwithstanding, this rose blazed a path for polyanthas and was used many times, directly and indirectly, as a parent, thus helping to found a very successful branch of the rose family.

Mrs W. H. Cutbush (1907). 'Mme Norbert Levavasseur' sported to provide this fine variety. It has shiny foliage and strong growth. The semi-double, lightly scented flowers are deep pink. Strong stems support large clusters.

► **Petite Leonie** (1893). Raised by Soupert & Notting, this fine little rose has small, double blooms of pale pink fading to white. It has as its parents 'Mignonette' and 'Duke of Connaught'.

Petite Marcelle (1911). Dubreuil raised many roses and this little one is very worthwhile. It is white with some pink and has small, double flowers, freely produced on a low-growing plant.

▲ **Perle Orléanaise** (1913). Duveau produced this hybrid, which is a light pinkish-mauve of medium size, double, and grows to about 90 cm. Not seen very often these days.

Poulsen's Copper (1940). A rose with a spicy fragrance. The large double flowers can be 10 cm across and have shades of yellow, bronze, orange and pink in them at times. They are produced in profusion in clusters on a plant of medium height.

▼ **Poulsen's Crimson** (1950). Although this hybrid was introduced forty years ago, it still draws attention when in flower in the field. Its deep crimson, almost single blooms appear in upright clusters on a healthy plant. This rose, along with others in this group, was raised by the old-established firm of Poulsens of Denmark.

Founded in 1878 and introducing its first roses in 1912, this company has accomplished much valuable work in rose raising and had a dominant part in the founding of the hybrid polyantha class, which became a bridge between the old polyantha rose and the new floribunda rose. On a recent visit to the Poulsen Rosenplanteskole we were very graciously received by Pernille Olesen (Poulsen) who, with her husband, Mogens, is now the proprietor of this world-famous nursery. While walking through the grounds, the glasshouses and the rose fields, one could feel the sense of history and the love for roses which has been handed down from one generation to another. They, too, are working along new lines of endeavour with their new roses and there are many treasures coming for enthusiasts to see.

◄ **Poulsen's Yellow** (1938). It was quite an achievement to produce such a lovely yellow variety and this rose certainly stood out at the time of its introduction. The strongly scented blooms are of medium size, semi-double, and the plant grows to about 90 cm.

Rosalinde (1908). A variety raised by W. Paul, with small, double, pink flowers produced in clusters on a low, compact plant.

Tip Top (1909). Also known as 'Baby Doll', this unusual and beautiful rose comes from 'Trier' and a *R. foetida bicolor* seedling. A bushy, compact plant supports medium-sized, double flowers. They are rose-pink towards the edges and fade to white and lemon. A Peter Lambert hybrid.

Triomphe Orléanaise (1912). One of the brightest members of the group, this bears cherry-red, small, semi-double, lightly scented blooms which stand out in large clusters on a strong-growing plant.

▼ **Weisse Margot Koster** (1939). Many roses in many families have come into being because they sported or mutated from their parent. This useful rose has pure white, cupped flowers in clusters on a compact plant.

Pinkie

Climbers and their Hybrids

This collection of climbing roses is a real mixed bag. There are different types represented here which sometimes one finds difficult to accurately classify. There have been many enthusiasts, and one worthy of note was Alister Clark, of Glenara, near Melbourne. He worked industriously over many years, raising thousands of seedlings for little financial reward and often passing them on to non-profit organisations for distribution. He produced many types of roses, but in this section we are concerned only with some of his climbing roses.

He used as one parent a tremendous *Rosa gigantea* for many of his creations. He believed that this rose's great vigour was an essential attribute to pass on to his hybrids. Perhaps one could say that hardiness is another factor he should have sought. Many of Clark's roses are not hardy in the colder-climate countries, but they do live on majestically in warmer areas. Alister Clark, like many pioneers in other fields, was probably before his time. He carried out an extensive hybridising programme, breaking new ground, and it has taken the rest of the world a long time to catch up.

It is fitting to repeat his words, written in an article in the Melbourne *Herald* in October 1926, 'It is one of the most regrettable things in horticulture that the old roses of yesteryear, or even the last century, are allowed to go out of cultivation. I have had incredible difficulty in procuring such roses when seeking appropriate parents for new kinds. It is my practice to make almost yearly trips to New Zealand and I have been frequently abroad in my search for roses, and it has been a melancholy discovery that certain roses for which I have been in search are no longer to be had.' It is true, almost without saying, that words like these are reward enough for the collecting and preserving, at least for a time, of all the old varieties in our own living museum of roses. ∎

Alister Clark's garden

A Celebration of Old Roses

▲ **Countess of Stradbroke** (1928). Deep bright crimson, and very fragrant, large, globular flowers make this one of the most beautiful climbing roses you will see in a long time. Raised by Alister Clark, it has deep green foliage and is recurrent.
Doris Downes (1932). A very early flowerer, again raised by Alister Clark, this bears very large blooms, semi-double, cupped and strongly scented. The colour is medium-pink with deeper shadings and the growth quite vigorous.

▲ **American Beauty** (1909). Contrary to general belief, this rose is not a hybrid from the bush form. The fragrant, very large, deep rose-pink cupped blooms are produced profusely.
Auguste Roussell (1913). An unusual climber, quite beautiful in its own way. The petals are wavy, the colour combines shades of salmon and blush-pink, and the large, semi-double flowers are abundantly produced on a strong-growing plant.
► **Captain Christy** (1881). A fine climbing sport from the bush form. With parents like 'Victor Verdier' and 'Safrano', and the introducer being Ducher, it would have been disappointing if this rose was not a good one. Soft pink, double blooms of deeper colour in the middle.
Chastity (1924). A once-flowering variety that is well worth growing. The blooms, pure white with lemon at the base, are large, very fragrant and have high, pointed centres.

Flying Colours (1922). Another Clark hybrid, raised from the tremendous *R. gigantea* plant in his garden. It has a light scent and large, single flowers of deep pink to light red. Extremely strong-growing and non-recurrent.

▲ **Frau Karl Druschki** (1906). Also known as 'Reine des Neiges', 'Snow Queen', and 'White American Beauty', all names used for political purposes. It has been said by more than one enthusiast that if this rose had been graced with a scent, its popularity would not have declined. Large, pure white, well-shaped blooms.

Glory of California (1935). Alister Clark raised this hybrid which has light-pink, medium-sized, double blooms with a nice scent. It is quite vigorous and healthy.

Kitty Kininmonth (1922). This too was raised from *R. gigantea* by Clark. It has been a very popular climber for many years, with its semi-double, very large, cupped blooms of bright deep pink with golden stamens. Extremely vigorous and healthy.

La Follette (1910). This, too, is a *R. gigantea* hybrid, this time raised by Busby. It resembles 'Belle of Portugal', but is softer in its colour tonings. Like its relations, it is not completely hardy and only thrives in milder climates.

Mme Segond Weber (1911). A fine sport from the bush form which was raised by Soupert & Notting in 1907. Long stems support well-shaped, large flowers of pale salmon-pink. They are fragrant and produced profusely.

Miss Marion Manifold (1913). A lovely deep red, velvety, fragrant rose with large, double, globular flowers on a strong plant with large leathery leaves.

Mrs Aaron Ward (1922). One of the main features of this variety is its variability. The double flowers are yellow and salmon and so seem to change shades at times. It has long pointed buds.

Mrs W. J. Grant (1899). 'Belle Siebrecht'. This fine rose came from 'La France' and 'Lady Mary Fitzwilliam', which probably explains its popularity over a long period. The blooms are double, light pink and fragrant.

▼ **Ophelia** (1920). The bush 'Ophelia' was introduced by Paul in 1912 and this photograph shows a climbing form. Many a florist owes much to the high quality, fragrant, pale salmon, blush and lemon flowers produced by this variety over thirty years. Ideal for floral artistry work.

Peggy Ann Landon (1938). One of the many fine roses raised by the Brownells. A very strong-growing plant, it has large, fragrant flowers which are a light lemon and apricot.

▲ **Pinkie** (1952). Although this rose is really not an old one, it is a delightful variety which has an 'old' look about it. One of its parents is 'China Doll'. This rose bears lightly double blooms, abundantly presented. They are bright pink with a touch of carmine. 'Pinkie' can have a very good late flowering. This climber has few thorns.

▲ **Pink Mermaid** (1960). This rose is a mystery in that no one seems to know anything about its parentage or, for that matter, where it came from. I understand it originated in California, possibly in the Palo Alto area, where I have seen it growing 10–12 metres up a tree. Upon close examination there is a distinct possibility that this hybrid does have some 'Mermaid' in it. The flowers are single and about 8 cm across, with petals which have gaps between them and look quite clematis-like. They appear profusely and in clusters in a grand flowering and there is quite a lot of intermittent bloom later. The foliage is handsome and quite vigorous; the stems are long and slender and can be quite wispy and supple. There are thorns, but not many, and they are large and hooked, just like those of its suspected parent. The colour is basically pink, with cream and lemon shades towards the centre, and the freshly opened flower has some pale salmon in it. All in all, when in full bloom this rose can be quite beautiful. It has been suggested that there may be some 'Tausendschön' somewhere in its parentage.

Princeps (1942). A very useful rose, again raised by Clark. This variety is not too vigorous and really could be considered more of a pillar rose. It is non-repeating, with large crimson-scarlet blooms which are nicely fragrant.

Queen of Hearts (1920). Here Alister Clark departed from his favourite *R. gigantea* and used 'Gustav Grunerwald' and 'Rosy Morn' to produce this lovely hybrid. Rich-pink, double, fragrant flowers and a long flowering season.

Red New Dawn (1956). 'Étendard'. A hybrid between 'New Dawn' and an unnamed seedling. Big clusters of bright red, fragrant, medium blooms are produced profusely on a strong-growing plant which has shiny foliage.

Scorcher (1922). A 'Mme Abel Chatenay' seedling which flowers very freely. The scarlet-crimson blooms are 8 cm or more across and semi-double. Vigorous growth, healthy plant and free-flowering. Another Clark hybrid.

It may seem to the reader that this family has been a special promotion for Alister Clark, of Melbourne but this is not the way things were intended. In each rose field of endeavour, in almost every country of the world, there have been hybridists working quietly along their own particular lines of interest. Alister Clark was one of these men.

Souvenir de Mme Boullet (1930). One of the most popular roses raised by Pernet-Ducher. Long, pointed buds opening to deep yellow, large flowers of good shape, over a long season.

Squatter's Dream (1923). Deep to medium-yellow, semi-double, very fragrant, large flowers which pale with age. The wood is without thorns and the foliage is deep green and shiny.

▼ **Tenor** (1963). Although this variety is comparatively modern, it does fit in well here. We saw it in Le Parc de Bagatelle in Paris where there are several lovely examples of it. The blooms appear in quite big clusters, are semi-double, velvety-crimson and produced in great numbers.

◄ **Weisse New Dawn** (1959). When you consider what a good all-round performer 'New Dawn' is, now that we have a pure white colour sport of it, we are indeed lucky. To be able to plant them adjacently and enjoy the beauty of the same plant and growth with the two separate colours is almost more than one could have hoped for.

White Maman Cochet (1907). Obviously a climbing sport from the bush form, a grand old rose which was introduced in 1896. It is very nice to have a climbing form available. Double, cupped blooms of white, sometimes flushed pink.

Immensee

Ramblers and their Relatives

One would have thought that after the groups of ramblers that were written about in my first two books it would not be possible to assemble another batch of at least equal usefulness and beauty. One point should be made clear. When these roses are brought from the Northern Hemisphere it has become apparent that, although they are described as once-flowering in countries like Germany and Denmark, many of them will flower again in the southern climate of Australasia.

The rambling family comes from quite a few sources, and sometimes it is difficult to decide if a rose really belongs to the ramblers or should be classified as a climber. A variety can have the best of breeding and to all intents and purposes should be a rambler, but sometimes it might not make the necessary tall growth. Then again, another variety can have the best climbing background but looks more like a rambler than you would think possible. These roses are mostly from *R. wichuraiana* and *R. sempervirens*, but there are also some from *R. setigera*, *R. multiflora* and *R. arvensis*, as well as others.

We, the present-day rose growers, can find that, as with all the families of roses, particular people were involved with different hybridisation programmes, and it is to these enthusiasts that we must be grateful. Many well-known names we are already familiar with, but how many know of the works of early American hybridists Prince, Feast, Horvath and Walsh, and also Dawson and Van Fleet? At the same time we should not forget the work of Thomas and the Brownells. Some roses raised by these hybridists have already been dealt with in the previous volumes and some are in the group that follows. ∎

Aunt Harriet (1918). A fine rambler from Van Fleet, this is a vigorous, healthy grower which has big clusters of bright crimson-scarlet, large flowers with a distinctive white eye and yellow stamens. They are double and nicely scented.

Beauty of the Prairies (1843). This fine rose is a *R. setigera* hybrid raised by Feast. It is a very hardy variety which has rounded, large, fragrant, double flowers of a lovely bright pink which sometimes shows a white stripe.

▲ **Clematis** (1924). An unusual and interesting variety which is vigorous and quite distinctive. It has quite small flowers which are single and deep red with a lighter area in the centre. They appear in large clusters on a healthy plant.

▲ **Copper Glow** (1940). One of the family raised by the Brownells. It is double, quite large in the flower and of the prettiest orange-copper shading. The plant is rather loose or open and the flowers are very fragrant and profuse.

A Celebration of Old Roses

▲ **Coronation** (1911). I have to wonder why this variety is not better known. It has bright scarlet, double flowers in clusters. They sometimes show white markings. The blooms are about medium size and appear profusely on a healthy plant.

▼ **Crème** (1895). This rambler is a very pretty cream and white, small-flowered variety which has fragrant blooms produced in great numbers. Its lovely daisy-like blossoms are unusual and of a type which I have seen only once before.

▲ **Dunkelröte Tausendschön**
(1942). Everyone knows how
extremely pretty and useful
'Tausendschön' is as a rambler.
This hybrid is a deep-red-
coloured sport of this beautiful
rose. Apart from its colour, it
is the same as its parent in
every respect.
▼ **Eisenach** (1909). A little-
known rose which takes its name
from a beautiful old East German
city just over the border from
Frankfurt. It is vigorous, and
bears large clusters of single,
small and deep red flowers with
a lemon centre.

▲ **Declic** (1988). Very new and
quite modern in its colour of
smoky lavender-grey, although
old in its style of small,
rounded flowers which appear
in clusters. I have seen this
variety only in Le Parc de
Bagatelle rose garden in Paris,
where it is in excellent
company.
Donna Marie (1830). An old
variety raised by Vibert. This
beautiful oldtimer has a
tremendous display of quite
small, cupped, very double
creamy-white flowers in large
clusters. It is fragrant and has
quite a good late flowering as
well.
Dr Huey (1914). Deep red,
semi-double, medium-sized
flowers on a vigorous plant.
This variety is known in the
United States as 'Shafter' and is
used there and in several other
countries as a rootstock. It is
lightly fragrant and has a
healthy growth.

A Celebration of Old Roses

Fernand Tanne (1920). This, too, is not so well known, but it is a beautiful rose. It is very fragrant, with flowers of deep yellow early, then creamy-yellow later. The flowers are large and double, and the growth healthy and prolific.

► **Frau Albert Hochstrasser** (1908). Small, pink and lemon, double blooms grace this healthy, happy-looking plant in clusters. They are nicely scented and contrast well with the glossy, deep green foliage with light brown young growth.

▼ **Helene** (1897). Raised by Lambert, this variety has the prettiest of colour combinations in its little more than single blooms which come in very large clusters. They are lightly

scented and have shades of white, cream, lemon, pink, violet, mauve and rose, all of which are light in their intensity. A beautiful old hybrid.

▼ **Hiawatha Recurrent** (1931). The name of this rose seems to imply that it is a sport from 'Hiawatha', but this is not so. There is some resemblance, but the colour is different, being a blend of orange and carmine with white in the centre. It does flower later, and it is vigorous and has shiny foliage.

► **Immensee** (1984). This hybrid, raised by Kordes, is quite new but does have an old look about it. It has medium-sized, bright pink, single blooms with golden stamens in large clusters, and the growth is very strong. Excellent for groundcover. Also known as 'Grouse'.

Jacotte (1920). A Barbier hybrid which is very much up to his usual high standard. The semi-double, 8 cm flowers open nicely, are bronzy-yellow with coppery-red tonings, and the growth is very vigorous with shiny, deep green foliage.

▲ **Long John Silver** (1934). One of Horvath's seedlings which is very vigorous and quite hardy. It has very large blooms in large clusters. They are cupped and well scented and silvery white. The foliage is leathery and strong growing.

Mary Lovett (1915). This Van Fleet hybrid is a fine example of this hybridist's work. Its large, double, nicely fragrant blooms are the whitest white. The plant is vigorous and healthy.

Mosel (1920). A fine hybrid from two fine parents in 'Mme Norbert Levavasseur' and 'Trier', the former a polyantha, the latter a hybrid musk. Trier is a beautiful city nestled on the banks of the Mosel. Raised by Peter Lambert, this rose is double, lightly scented and violet-blue with a reddish centre.

A Celebration of Old Roses

Nanette (1926). It seems that now and again a rose which is not well known pops up on the scene and it really is a fine variety. This one has clusters of large, creamy-white, strongly scented double flowers.

Newport Fairy (1908). Also known as 'Newport Rambler'. There have been many roses raised from 'Crimson Rambler' and another parent, in this case *R. wichuraiana*, which gives this hybrid its glossy foliage. Deep rosy-pink, small, single flowers, lighter in the centre.

Pink Roamer (1898). Another Horvath hybrid which is from *R. wichuraiana* and 'Cramoisi Supérieure'. A strong-growing plant supports plentiful clusters of white-centred, single, pink flowers.

Princesse Louise (1828). This variety and the following one are very old. Both were raised by Jacques and both are hybrids of *R. sempervirens*. Pale pink, very double, large flowers with a muddled centre.

► **Princesse Marie** (1829). The breeder, Jacques, is perhaps better known for raising 'Adelaide d'Orléans' and 'Félicité et Perpétué', two beautiful and excellent ramblers. This variety has large clusters of medium-sized, double, pink flowers.

▼ **Queen Alexandra** (1915). Small, single, pink blooms with a white centre in large clusters appear on a vigorous healthy plant. (Not to be confused with the hybrid tea rose of similar name.)

▲ **Repandia** (1982). Also known as 'Partridge'. Bright pink, single flowers in large clusters on a vigorous plant which is ideal for groundcover. There is also a white form of it which is just as beautiful.

Romeo (1919). Produced by Easlea, this hybrid is quite strong growing and produces a fine display of nicely shaped, double, crimson-scarlet blooms in smallish clusters.

Ruby Queen (1900). *R. wichuraiana* is one of the parents of this lovely hybrid produced by Van Fleet. Lightly scented, deep rose-pink, small, double blooms in clusters of three or more on a plant to about 3 metres.

Source d'Or (1913). A once-flowering, beautiful variety, raised by Turbat. The blooms are very fragrant, bronzy-yellow with a lighter edge, and double and large, in clusters.

Sweet Lavender (1912). This is an English hybrid raised by W. Paul. Small, single, blush-pink and light mauve flowers in large clusters on a strong-growing plant.

Troubadour (1911). Mainly once-flowering, this Walsh variety has dark, shiny foliage on a vigorous-growing plant. The double, bright-red blooms have a wine shade at times and appear in clusters.

Unique (1928). A very nice coppery-orange-salmon repeat-flowering hybrid which seems to have been discarded too soon. It is a strong grower and the flowers are medium sized and double.

▶ **Venusta Pendula** (1928). *R. arvensis* is one of the parents of this fine rose. It is a very strong grower and a very profuse flowerer. The blooms are blush-pink, medium sized and double.

Wedding Bells (1906). To conclude this group, another Walsh hybrid. It has pink, semi-double blooms with a white centre and they come in clusters on a strong, healthy plant.

Gertrude Jekyll

English Roses

In my second book it was my pleasure to introduce the reader to David Austin's English roses. Beautiful they certainly are and enduring they must surely be for, as predicted, these roses, which capture parts of the new and the old, are becoming very popular. It seems that their charm and usefulness are going to be recognised everywhere. True, some of them will not thrive in particular places, but is this not the same with numerous other roses? It is significant and important that the demand for these English roses is rapidly increasing among growers around the world.

The interest in David Austin's roses and the manner in which this English raiser has gone about creating them is now being copied by other hybridists in different countries. This is a compliment to the original raiser of the family, and, no matter what happens in the future, it was David Austin who started it all. His path, like that of all trail-blazers, has never been easy, but recognition for his work is now apparent. No doubt this work will go on for many years, and the family of English roses will live on as a memorial to the man who had the courage to bring his ideas into reality against all the odds.

It is my prediction that this family, along with others now being created, will inevitably supersede the present-day modern roses, which for some years now have been losing their identity. Rose societies will have to take a long, hard look at themselves and ask the question, why have they shut out other types of roses from their shows and displays for so many years? In the future, without high-pointed hybrid teas and large-flowered floribundas to worship, I wonder what will make up the

classes at the shows. Is it too much to ask that hundreds of years and thousands of varieties of old roses should at last be recognised?

Among the group to follow, which are all fine roses, are two which are different. 'Winchester Cathedral' is a sport from that excellent variety, 'Mary Rose', and this opportune happening of Nature has presented us with a most beautiful white rose. White roses in all forms are always popular and this one has all the attributes needed. Fragrant, and freely branching, it produces flowering wood quickly and grows into a neat, rounded shrub.

'Wildflower' is a true single of only five petals. The flowers come in groups of three or

more, and although the individual bloom does not seem to last long, another soon takes over from it. The buds are buttery-yellow and the freshly opened flower is yellow fading to cream. It has a strong fragrance and a compact habit which would make it an excellent variety for a low hedge or border. ■

▼ **Abraham Darby** (1985). A larger variety which will grow to 2 metres, with a rounded habit and lovely arching branches with large, double blooms. These are sumptuous to say the least, with a strong fruity fragrance. They can be 10-12 cm across and their colour is a pleasing mix of pink, salmon, lemon and apricot.

Autumn Leaves (1981). Healthy, upright growth is the hallmark of this unusual rose. It seems to be tallish in habit and has large, distinctive petals of a muddled nature. The flowers are cream in the bud, which colour is retained on the edges when the blooms open to varying shades of reddish-pink and amber. Quite striking when seen at its best.

Charles Rennie Mackintosh (1988). Named after the extraordinary Scottish architect and designer. A very fragrant, small to medium-sized shrub with tough, thorny growth. It is very hardy. The cupped flowers of lilac-pink are of medium size and freely produced.

Claire Rose (1986). This has majestic flowers of blush-pink which pale to creamy-white when fully open. The very double blooms are fragrant and open flat on a strong, upright, very healthy plant with pale green leaves.

Dr Jackson (1987). At first sight you might liken this rose to

'Scarlet Fire' but it really has several differences. It produces its single, bright crimson-scarlet blooms in great profusion. The flowers are medium-sized on a healthy shrub and these are followed by a fine crop of fruit.

▲ **Emanuel** (1985). Free-flowering and strongly fragrant, this rose was named for Elizabeth and David Emanuel, the designers of Princess Diana's wedding dress. Its large blooms are a pleasant mixture of pink, salmon and lemon. They are quartered and flat, typical of the English rose attributes.

English Elegance (1986). Arching branches on a strong healthy plant support quite large flowers which open wide. Each bloom has a loosely arranged, almost muddled, centre and is coloured in several different shades of blush-pink, pink, salmon and bronze. Altogether a very lovely combination.

◄ **English Garden** (1986). It is pleasing to see yellow coming to the fore in this family. Lightly fragrant, this rose makes an excellent bedding variety because of its compact growth. Pale green foliage contrasts with the flat, open flowers which are a soft apricot-yellow in the middle, paling towards lemon on the outer.

▲ **Financial Times Centenary** (1988). Bourbon-like in its appearance. It has large, cupped, strongly fragrant blooms of a glowing deep pink. It was named to commemorate the 100th anniversary of the famous pink newspaper. Upright strong growth and deep green foliage.

▼ **Fisherman's Friend** (1987) Deep garnet-red and cerise-crimson are the changing colours of this beautiful rose. Flat, very double large flowers are produced on a strong-growing, thorny plant. Powerful scent.

▼ **Francine Austin** (1988). A real break from the accepted form of English roses. Although this variety is quite new, it could be taken for an old one. Its habit is procumbent, growth healthy and it has excellent bright green foliage. The flowers are small, about 5 cm across, rosette type and of the purest white. They appear in rambler-like sprays over a long flowering period.

A Celebration of Old Roses

▲ **Gertrude Jekyll** (1986). If you have never watched a rose develop from the bud to the open flower, this is the one to watch. Rich pink colour and a very strong fragrance, along with its upright, healthy growth, make this a very exciting rose.

◄ **L. D. Braithwaite** (1988). We saw this rose in David Austin's field in July 1988, and again at the Festival of the Rose at St Albans, and if it lives up to its early promise it will be the largest rose we have ever seen. As witnessed on the two occasions already mentioned, one bloom would cover a saucer. It is of the deepest crimson and has a very strong fragrance.

▲ **Othello** (1986). Robust, healthy growth and dense, deep green foliage support lusty, cupped blooms of dusky crimson which, with age, change to purple and mauve. This rose has a very powerful fragrance and would help to make excellent pot-pourri.

Potter & Moore (1988). Roses can be named for all manner of reasons, and this beautiful rose was given its name to mark the introduction of Potter & Moore's 'Rose' range of toiletries. For an established business, founded in 1749, this is a very appropriate rose. It has medium-pink, quartered, double blooms with a very good fragrance.

A Celebration of Old Roses

▲ **Queen Nefertiti** (1988). When this variety becomes known it will also become very popular, by reason of its fragrance, its bushy growth and its very lovely blooms of soft yellow and pale apricot. The attractive, compact plant seems to flower continuously.

► **Saint Cecilia** (1987). Fragrance seems to be the hallmark of this family and this fine rose carries on the tradition. Its exquisitely shaped, bourbon-like flowers are creamy-buff, cupped, and produced evenly over a healthy, medium-sized plant. A must for those who would like the best of both worlds.

This rose gets its name from a fifth-century legend, which tells that Cecilia was a Roman aristocrat who vowed to retain her virginity despite being forced to marry the nobleman Valerean. He agreed to respect her wishes and he and his brother Tiburtius were granted the vision of an angel. Shortly afterwards all three were martyred, Cecilia being beheaded. It was in the fifteenth century that St Cecilia was adopted as patron by various musical guilds. She is represented as playing the organ, and her feast day is 22 November.

◄ **Sir Walter Raleigh** (1985). A pleasing fragrance from a very large flower of clear, warm pink with an open centre showing golden stamens. The plant develops well with large healthy foliage. In David Austin's words, 'named to commemorate the founding of the English-speaking colony in America'.

Swan (1987). If you are looking for a tough white rose for all conditions, this could be the one. A strong, tall-growing shrub bearing magnificent large, white blooms with buff shades when it first opens. Quite fragrant, flat rosettes with petals reflexing.

► **Symphony** (1986). The attractive, large, flat rosette-type flowers of medium-yellow in the centre, paling to cream at the edges, are borne on a healthy plant which has light green foliage. With all this, it has a lovely fragrance as well.

▼ **The Countryman** (1987). Bright rose-pink, many petalled flowers in profusion. This variety has a double ration of portland rose in it, and a strong old-rose fragrance. The plant grows wider than tall and would be excellent in any shrubbery.

A Celebration of Old Roses

The Nun (1987). Lightly scented, deeply cupped, semi-double white flowers, at times with a resemblance to a tulip bloom. The stamens are often visible. Very free-flowering, on arching sprays, this is a useful addition to the family.

► **Warwick Castle** (1986). Named to commemorate the reopening of the Victorian rose garden at Warwick Castle. The lovely, wispy, arching branches of this variety make it look as if it would climb quite easily. The blooms are large and very double, opening into a flat rosette of a deep, glowing pink. This beautiful variety is deeply scented.

Wildflower (1986). A useful rose which can be used for borders or bedding. It has single, buttery-yellow blooms of medium size which pale after opening. They are fragrant and flowers are produced in clusters in great profusion.

▼ **William Shakespeare** (1987). This variety was produced from a cross between 'The Squire' and 'Mary Rose', two excellent roses in their own right. Perhaps it has some of the attributes of both — the colour of the one and the form of the other. Deep crimson, gallica-like blooms are large, many petalled and flat. They are freely produced on strong-growing shrubs with dark green foliage.

▲ **Winchester Cathedral** (1988). There are times when a hybridist's skills are not required and this white rose is a fine example of Nature's handiwork. It is a sport from 'Mary Rose' and is identical to it in every way except in its colour. Excellent white roses are always well sought after and I have no doubt this one will be very popular, too.

PART THREE

Changes for your Garden

Oh, Adam was a gardener,
  and God who made him sees
That half a proper gardener's work
  is done upon his knees,
So when your work is finished,
  you can wash your hands and pray
For the Glory of the Garden,
  that it may not pass away!
And the Glory of the Garden,
  it shall never pass away.

Rudyard Kipling (1865-1936)

Castle Howard garden

Changes for your Garden

We have now come to the final section of this volume and I find it quite difficult to decide what to write about when I feel there really is so much yet to discuss. We should not sit back smugly and mistakenly think we know it all. I am reminded of a lady from overseas who visited us a few years ago. She said she had been involved with old roses for several years and would like to look at our collection. A couple of hours later she was ready to leave and handed me a list of roses she considered wrongly named. Whatever happened to the meek and the mild?

As already stated in these books, when it comes to the identification of old roses there are so many imponderables. For one reason or another, roses have been given names, and for all we know the name could be the correct one or the wrong one. Apart from the few whose names are generally agreed upon, how do we really know about the others. I would suggest that those who put a name to a rose for some flimsy reason or other, without any degree of certainty when there really can be no degree of certainty, are the ones causing the most confusion. Another factor, which has been mentioned before, is the prolific manner in which many of the really old roses grow from seed. The fact that a rose never had a name does not seem to stop some people showing their 'expertise' by giving it one. There is little need for me to explain the confusion that this malpractice leads to. The identification of an old rose will, and must always, be a very difficult proposition.

Leaving behind the question of 'a rose by any other name', we should once again address the subject of using the excellent climbing shrub and rambling roses in every conceivable way. It seems that these days old garden favourites such as camellias, azaleas and rhododendrons have become very popular, and they too have had their image changed. A much wider variety of colour, size and type can now be obtained, but in spite of all the work done in this quarter, the length of these shrubs' flowering season has not really been extended. When you come to think of it, there really are not many flowering shrubs of any kind which flower much past mid summer. This is where the shrub roses, climbers and ramblers have so much to recommend them.

Although you may have heard it before, a shrub rose is one which grows about as tall as it grows wide. It also has the inherent ability to flower all over, even to the ground. Although the earliest families are very old and mostly have but one annual flowering season, there are at least twice as many which are not so old and will flower again and again. Some varieties even do this while producing attractive, showy fruit.

What could be better than thinking of these roses as flowering shrubs and placing them among your mostly once-flowering evergreen shrubs. Here they will add much colour and scent to your garden in a most attractive way.

The choice of varieties, of course, is always a personal thing. I am often asked what I recommend for a special place, be it a pillar, a fence, a wall or just in the garden. My answer will always be that the person asking the question should really make the choice. I feel strongly that our work lies in the collecting, propagation and distribution of these wonderful roses. In doing this we learn to appreciate them all. The customer has the very difficult task of settling on one rose for one place, and this choice must necessarily be his or hers. We can *suggest* many roses for a particular place, but the final choice for that special area should be made preferably after seeing them in flower. After all, it is your garden and you will be looking at and enjoying this rose for years to come.

Not only the lovely shrub roses can be used to add colour to the greener areas of your garden. Ramblers are also suitable and they can give extra height as well.

If you carefully study the photographs in this section you will realise what a beautiful creation you can very easily place in almost any spot in your garden. Firstly you must, of course, choose the rambling rose you would like. Plate i shows a fine specimen of 'Lykkefund' growing on a metal pole. There are two ways to achieve this effect.

Plate i

A Celebration of Old Roses

Plate ii

Often we have planted a rambler without support because the metal pole was not available at the time, and it has grown happily along the ground for one or two seasons until the 4-metre pole was ready. Then the long growths were gathered from their flat-growing situation and held up against the metal stake while at least three wire twitches were applied to loosely bind the lush growth to the support. The other method is to drive the 4-metre stake at least 1 metre into the ground and then simply plant and grow the rose up this support. It seems you get a more immediate and dramatic effect from the first method.

Plate ii shows a very fine example of a rose which has apparently been around for some years now. As it shows some affinity with 'Mermaid', it is called 'Pink Mermaid'. It is a vigorous grower and will easily cover a pole in two seasons. What could be more beautiful than a specimen like this gracing your garden and giving height to a flat area? People often say to me, 'But I have no room left in my garden.' Yes, you have, you know — up in the sky.

Plate iii shows a comparatively young plant of a beautiful rambler called 'Madelaine Selzer' which has just recently come my way. It has quite large, double blooms which are lemon in the bud and open creamy-white. They are produced freely and have a nice scent. All three of the illustrated examples are quite beautiful in their own right, and there are plenty more to choose from.

When considering roses for pillars and poles, we must not forget the pillar roses themselves, or even the noisettes. Plate iv shows an excellent 'Joseph's Coat' growing more than happily in the rose garden in Le Parc de Bagatelle in Paris. There is no reason why varieties such as 'Hamburger Phoenix', 'Ilse Kröhn Superior', 'Clair Matin' and many others cannot be trained the same way for all the reasons mentioned earlier. It is generally agreed that a pillar rose will eventually reach 2 or more metres high, but will do so in a more sedate manner than a rambler. This type of rose may take longer to establish, but once the framework of growing wood is in place, you really have something to

Plate iii

Plate iv

Plate vi

behold. The many changing colours of a rose such as that shown in Plate iv are quite spectacular.

Again, in Plate v a more recent variety called 'Parure d'Or' shows its extreme beauty and the height which it may attain. There are many such pillar, pole and tripod roses in the famous gardens in the Bois de Boulogne, and not least of these is 'Izeran', shown in Plate vi. I cannot find this rose listed, but I can assure you that even without flowers it is a most interesting and striking plant. The leaves are large, unusually shaped and deep green, reminiscent perhaps of a large-leafed ivy.

For those readers, who for one reason or another, do not want to bother with any of the foregoing roses to light up their gardens, there is another alternative. This involves using a weeping standard rose which, of course, is no more than a suitably selected rambling rose grafted on to a tall rootstock, from something less than 2 metres to anything over this height which is practicable. If using one of these, you will require a good stake, but upon planting, the effect is almost immediate and because a standard rose has a clean stem, it can be underplanted or planted reasonably close to other shrubs and plants. Plates vii and viii show two excellent examples of these beautiful and useful weeping standards. In Japan, the weeping standards are grown to over 3 metres, and what a magnificent sight they are.

Plate v

Plate vii

Plate viii

'Paul Transon' is the beautiful rose shown in Plate vii and this variety is all that you could wish for. It has large, fragrant, double blooms of an unusual shade of salmon-pink, with petals which seem to be quilled at times. The flowers are freely produced along the length of the arching branches, once established, and there is quite a lot of late flower, too. The foliage is very glossy and medium green; the growth is coppery-bronze with a purplish hue. All in all, a fascinating rose which cannot help but give good service.

The rose shown in Plate viii is 'Sea Foam', which is not really a rambling rose, and not usually grown as a standard, but certainly makes a fine weeping specimen. This rose has a procumbent or lax habit of growth in its natural state, so when grown high up on a standard, at first it will be slow to develop because it does not have the long rambling growths, but later it will reach down, and it makes the most delightful sight. Although 'Sea Foam' commences flowering later in the season than most others of this type, when it does break into blossom it has the ability to flower almost continuously right through to winter. The blooms are medium sized, in clusters

of rosette shape, coloured blush-pink on opening but soon becoming white, and it is fragrant. What more could you ask from a variety that you could easily have in your garden?

Should your garden be one where you need some form of privacy or shelter, or both, then perhaps you could consider a rose hedge. Not a hedge in the sense of a trimmed row of conifers or other plants, but a hedge in the sense of a free-standing row of shrub roses or a row of roses trained more or less flat along a wire fence about 1.5 metres high. Plates ix and x show two hedges of hybrid musks supported by a wire fence at the Royal Horticultural Society's gardens at Wisley, south of London. Look carefully at these two photographs and you will see roses in lovely pastel shades which are more often in flower than not and would provide the best possible background or privacy screen for your garden. This type of rose is comparatively trouble-free from pests and diseases, and most varieties are not very thorny. There are many other rose varieties which would make an excellent free-standing hedge or privacy screen. Species, rugosas, bourbons, teas, albas, damasks, polyanthas and chinas are some of the families which include many examples of good roses for this purpose.

Plate xi is a view of part of our display garden in Temuka. It is placed here to give you some idea of the use of roses as bright spots in gardens where the colour may have passed. In the foreground is the very good 'Röte Max Graf' with its prolific single, bright crimson flowers. The plant grows in a procumbent manner and will reach 3 or more metres across. To the right of the picture you will notice a large shrub with pink, semi-double flowers. This is 'Applejack', which grows to about 2 metres high and across and is abundant in its flowering. In front of it stands a young weeping standard, 'Paul Transon', which in due time will grow into a

Plate ix

Plate x

lovely specimen with blooms right down to the ground. At the rear of the photograph is a picket fence supporting two rambling roses, 'Old Danish' on the left and 'The Garland' on the right. The former is a fine old rose which has double, bright pink, medium-to-large blooms in one long flowering season. 'The Garland' has large clusters of small, daisy-like, creamy-white flowers in profusion. Both are quite fragrant. If you can imagine roses like these in your garden, then I must be happy.

When you study Plates xii and xiii, remember they were taken in Le Parc de Bagatelle. Although what you see may be too grand for you, my reason for placing them here is so that you could modify them to suit your own situation. The overhead arches and the chains between posts are ideal for rambling roses and their flexible growth. You may have an entrance way to the lawn, or into your garden, where you could place two poles with a crosspiece on top. Plant two ramblers on the poles and watch for the change in the entrance way. Then again, you may have a curved or straight bed or pathway where you could place poles at 3-metre intervals. At about 2-metre height chains or rope can be attached so that they sag nicely between the poles. Rambling roses can then be planted at the base of the pole and they can be systematically guided up each one and along the chains as shown in Plate xiii. They are not difficult to train and, apart from removing unwanted growths and some old wood from time to time, the work is not time-consuming. There are many fine varieties for you to choose from, including 'Bobbie James', 'Shower of Gold', 'Dunkelröte Tausendschön' and 'Auguste Gervais'.

I hope you will agree with me that there are many ways in which you can change the look of your garden by using roses. Lack of space precludes me detailing all the methods available to give your garden height and colour, but at

Plate xii

least I have given you some ideas on how to use roses for this purpose.

We have now come to the end of this fascinating journey through another tremendous field of old roses. I trust you will have learned from it, as I have. We must not be smug with our knowledge but must always allow for the fact that we could be wrong. Has it ever occurred to you that the roses themselves could not care less if they have a name or not, and this is just another instance of humans imposing on Nature? From all of my efforts over many years we have met some wonderful people and had some tremendous experiences and this we feel is reward enough.

Perhaps it would be appropriate to allow my friends Dawn and Derek Bailey to have the last word. I had the pleasure of visiting Great Britain in 1984 and stayed with the Baileys in Little Thetford, near Ely, in Cambridgeshire. I had time on my hands and Dawn was keen to do something with the outside of their home but did not quite know where to begin. This paragraph is from a letter sent to me in June 1989:

'I do hope you realise, Trevor, that you have a lot to answer for. We have become obsessed with

Plate xi

Plate xiii

our garden, but we both agree it is a "magnificent obsession" from which we hope never to recover. At the moment the garden is looking most beautiful, with the best yet to come. Everything is early this year because of the mild winter and the warmest May for a hundred years. Of all the lovely plants and shrubs we have, for us nothing compares with the roses, and we will not rest until they are growing and climbing everywhere, and flowering amongst the shrubs and flowers. I do love to see them amongst the shrubs!'

Trevor Griffiths' display garden

Index

A Celebration of Old Roses